101 Great Resumes

By
Career Press editors

CAREER PRESS
3 Tice Road
P.O. Box 687
Franklin Lakes, NJ 07417
1-800-CAREER-1
201-848-0310 (NJ and outside U.S.)
FAX: 201-848-1727

101 GREAT RESUMES

ISBN 1-56414-201-9, $9.99

Cover design by The Gottry Communications Group, Inc.

Printed in the U.S.A. by Book-mart Press

To order this title by mail, please include price as noted above, $2.50 handling per order, and $1.00 for each book ordered. Send to: Career Press, Inc., 3 Tice Road, P.O. Box 687, Franklin Lakes, NJ 07417.

Or call toll-free 1-800-CAREER-1 (NJ and Canada: 201-848-0310) to order using VISA or MasterCard, or for further information on books from Career Press.

Library of Congress Cataloging-in-Publication Data

101 great resumes / by the editors of Career Press.
   p.   cm.
  Includes index.
  ISBN 1-56414-201-9 (pbk.)
  1. Resumes (Employment) I. Career Press Inc.
HF5383.A17   1996
808'.06665-dc20

95-50099
CIP

Contents

Part 1

How to write a resume

Chapter 1

Gathering courage... and information

As your fingers nimbly stroll through the yellow pages, searching for that ideal pet groomer or the nearest tire service, which advertisement catches your eye?

Most likely, it's the ad that is neat and well-organized. The wording is clear and concise. Perhaps a few well-placed graphics emphasize a point. White space helps avoid a cluttered look. And the ad contains information that specifically addresses your needs.

It seems that while your fingers were waltzing their way to Ted's Tire Service, they also stumbled on the essential elements of an effective resume.

You may never have envisioned it as such, but your resume is like a yellow pages ad, and you are the product. Just as that ad for Ted's Tire Service caught your attention and convinced you to give him a call, your resume must persuade a prospective employer that he or she needs your specific skills and experience. Like Ted, you must communicate that you have the goods...and can deliver.

You no doubt noticed other tire service ads, but none of them attracted your attention like Ted's.

So how can you make your resume stand out among all those other yellow pages ads on an employer's desk?

Read on!

Exactly what is a resume?

Quite simply put, a resume is a summary of your qualifications. In fact, the term comes from the French word *résumé*, which means "to summarize."

Your resume should describe you and show what you can do. It should include your professional and volunteer experience, special skills, education and accomplishments.

What will it do for me?

An excellent resume will not get you a job all on its own. But it does show you take you and your career seriously—that you've put time and thought into communicating your qualifications, accomplishments and goals.

A good resume helps you pique a prospective employer's interest and prevents you from achieving circular file status. Whether you're making a "cold" call or have already developed a contact within the company, your resume will help you market your skills and experience...and perhaps land you an interview

In today's job market, networking is essential. Your friends, neighbors, relatives and former co-workers are all significant contacts in the business world. Having a current resume comes in handy when Uncle James or Neighbor Nancy hears about a position right up your alley. Circulating your resume among your network increases your chances at gainful employment.

Your resume also serves as a self-assessment tool, an opportunity to complete a self-inventory and see where you've been and where you'd like to go. Creating your resume allows you to evaluate your career and set future goals.

What is an effective resume?

An effective resume must make a good first impression. Of course, appearance is important. Typos and crumpled paper do not go over well with prospective employers.

But content is even more crucial. The information in your resume needs to be well-organized, easy to read and results-oriented.

An effective resume should:

- **Address the employer's needs**. Think back to Ted's yellow pages ad. You called him because he convinced you that he could solve your particular problem. Employers hire people who can fill specific needs. Communicate that you are that person.

- **Show the employer how he/she will benefit**. Stress your accomplishments and show the employer you're an excellent prospect with talent to offer. Provide results-oriented data that proves you've handled previous jobs well and have consistently contributed to the success of the organization.

- **Be clear and concise**. Remember, employers sort through piles of resumes daily and typically devote about 30 seconds or less to each one. Make your information clear, concise and easy to read.

- **Organize you for the job search**. A good resume helps you focus on your accomplishments and career goals. It also helps organize your thoughts for potential job interviews. Once you've taken stock of yourself and realized all you've achieved and what you have to contribute, you'll enter the job interview and networking process with much more confidence.

Don't be intimidated

Writer's block. It rears its ugly head at the most inopportune times, and never as frequently as for the resume writer.

You're probably sitting there right now with a pencil or keyboard in hand, absolutely clueless, your mind a total blank.

It could be that you're a recent graduate who's just started your job search and have no idea where to begin. Perhaps you're reentering the work force after some time off and don't know how to explain that gap. Maybe you've been employed for 26 years and never *dreamed* at this point in your career you'd have to be marketing yourself to a new employer. Or perhaps you've decided to change careers and don't know how to apply your previous experience to your new career goal.

Whatever your situation, don't be intimidated by that blank piece of paper or computer screen. Actually, it would be nearly impossible at this point to sit down and write—on first try—a perfect resume. Actually, you shouldn't be writing anything. This is your "splat" time—the time to jot down any and everything that comes to mind when you think about your work and volunteer experience, your education, your special skills and your accomplishments.

Nobody said writing a resume was easy. Neither is giving birth or winning an Olympic medal. But the rewards are invaluable and worth all the effort.

Don't expect to finish this exercise in an hour or two. A well-prepared and well-written resume will take time and more than one draft. But if you follow the steps outlined in this book, your finished product will effectively present your skills and accomplishments, communicate benefits for the employer and address the employer's specific needs. Your reward: to be included in the pile of "possible candidates."

Gathering information

At this stage of the resume game, don't worry about having your information perfectly arranged and categorized. Don't even worry about having your entries in the right order. There are no extra points for organization right now. The immediate goal is to get your accomplishments and experience on a piece of paper. In the next chapter, you'll learn how to make order of this information and discover how to emphasize the qualifications and accomplishments you feel will be most meaningful to prospective employers.

For now, just "splat"—do a mind dump. Consider the following categories:

1. Work experience

Review all of your work experience, from baby-sitting for the neighbors to planning the marketing budget for a Fortune 500 company. Remember, everything counts, whether it was part-time or full-time employment.

Start off by listing the employer's name, location and your dates of employment. Ah, see? Now you've got something down on paper!

Responsibilities

Work on a brief description of your responsibilities, but don't go into too much detail—just consider your major functions and duties for each position. For example, if you're a sales manager applying with a new company, your prospective employer will be interested in knowing:

• How many people you supervised.

• If you managed a budget and, if so, its size.

• How much revenue you were responsible for.

• The size of your sales territory.

All of this information gives employers an idea of the responsibility you can handle. Consequently, it's especially important to consider those responsibilities that most apply to your chosen field or specific position.

Accomplishments

After summarizing your responsibilities, list your accomplishments and state them in specific terms.

What did you do on that job, and what were the results? Did you increase profit? Did you solve a problem? Did you exceed a goal? Did you improve product performance? Did you improve productivity or efficiency?

For example, suppose you're in sales, and you get a great idea on a way to expand a current market. You get the okay to implement it, and it turns out quite successfully. You could say:

• *Developed new sales program to expand established markets.*

But that leaves the employer hanging. He or she is no doubt questioning if the program ever got off the ground, and if it was successful.

Try this one instead:

• *Developed and implemented new sales program, which expanded three established markets by 35% and increased sales 55%.*

Now *that* says something! The entry becomes results-oriented and quantifies the achievement by including expansion and sales percentages.

You can't expect to have five entries like this for every job you've held, but be sure to carefully evaluate all your experience and include your specific achievements.

Here's another example: In two years, James has turned around a production section of the company's manufacturing plant. In addition, he's managed to exceed production schedules and objectives and turn out a nearly defect-free product, all while understaffed.

His entries read:

- *Exceeded production schedules while manufacturing a 99.5% defect-free product.*
- *Surpassed objectives while 15% understaffed.*

If you're having trouble identifying specific individual accomplishments, consider department or company-wide projects. Did your group supply the financial statistics that helped the research department determine whether the project would be a "go"? Did you serve on the team that evaluated your company's current computer system? Perhaps you found upgrading the systems would provide needed services and the company wouldn't have to buy a whole new system. Did your evaluation save the company money?

Also consider any work-related award that might reflect your accomplishments. Did you win an employee achievement award for writing the "New Employee Orientation Handbook"? Why? Was it because supervisors found that new employees who read the book had a better understanding of where they fit in and how they contributed to the company? That's an accomplishment! Don't leave it out!

A final, brief note on listing both responsibilities and accomplishments: As you begin to jot things down, don't begin your entries with "Responsible for." Instead, use an "action" word, such as *designed, created, directed, handled, achieved, supervised, coordinated* or *implemented.* These carry much more impact and truly describe what you did.

2. Volunteer experience

You don't have to be paid for your work for it to provide valuable experience.

For example, were you president of the Parent/Teacher Organization or band boosters last year? Did you plan and lead meetings? Did you organize and supervise the annual carnival fund raiser? Did you coordinate 50-some volunteers? Did you secure sponsors to help defray costs? Did your fund raiser see a profit? Sounds like some pretty good resume material!

It may not have occurred to you until now, but somewhere along the line you've probably managed the budget and purchasing for an organization's fund-raising supper, recruited volunteers for the library book sale or organized a musical program for the senior center. There was no pay for those jobs. But that doesn't mean they don't count.

If you have little or no paid work experience, or if you've been out of the job market and are preparing to reenter, your volunteer service translates well into work experience and should be included on your resume, along with any of your accomplishments with those organizations.

Be sure to write down the name of the organization, your volunteer service dates and your specific duties. As covered in the previous "work experience" section, focus on your accomplishments and quantify your results, if possible. Don't create entries that aren't true or are misleading, but be sure to take credit for your work.

For example, did your campaign drive for the women's symphony unit increase membership? How much? Did you serve on the committee that designed a community program on developing good parenting skills?

Then your entry might read:

- *Recommended and organized new women's symphony unit membership drive, which increased membership 35%.*

- *Designed, coordinated and presented "Developing Good Parenting Skills" program to fill a community need. Program has evolved into 150 volunteers and nearly 500 participants and earned state and county Division of Child and Family Services (Welfare) awards.*

Here's one final sample:

- *Created and organized first-ever PTO T-shirt sale, which brought in $1,500 to help purchase new elementary school playground equipment.*

Don't discount any contribution you may have made, even if you weren't in a leadership role. Maybe you recruited exhibitors for your sorority craft bazaar or drove senior citizens to their doctor appointments.

Employers want to hire productive people. Your volunteer service will show that you're an active person and enhance your chances of landing in the "possible candidate" file.

3. Education

For the most part, the educational listing is fairly brief. You'll want to include the name and location of the school, date of graduation and your degree or major area of study. If you didn't graduate, note the years you attended the school and the type of courses you completed. For example:

*   *Purdue University, West Lafayette, Ind., 20 credit hours in aeronautical engineering (1993-1995).*
*   *Courses in Elementary Education, University of Michigan, Ann Arbor, 1991-1992.*

If you're a recent high school, trade school or college graduate, you may want to list a few of the courses you completed, especially if you have little or no paid or volunteer work experience. But don't get too detailed. Just list those that apply to the position or field you're interested in.

Also, if you're short on work experience, play up your school activities and educational accomplishments. Perhaps you were president of the chess club or drum major for the band. Or maybe you performed an audit to fulfill a class requirement. Whatever the case, include the information and be specific about any of your accomplishments. For example:

*   *Led high school marching band to regional championship; won award for outstanding direction as drum major.*
*   *Recommended new schedule for Big Ten chess tournament, which reduced travel time and lost school hours.*
*   *Performed audit of company with 500 employees to fulfill class requirement; recommended new computerized bookkeeping software, which reduced data entry time and provided more detailed reports.*

When you actually begin to write your resume, you may decide this information is better presented elsewhere. But for now, just include it here.

You may also want to note special circumstances, such as achieving a high GPA while earning 60 percent of your college expenses. This proves you're a hard worker and take your education seriously...and shows employers you'd be a productive employee.

GPA, graduating with honors

If you've been employed for several years, your high school and college grades really are insignificant to a prospective employer. After 10 or 20 years in the work force, your experience and accomplishments should speak for themselves and prove you're productive and intelligent.

However, if you're recently out of school and your grades are good, feel free to include them in the educational section. Be sure to include the scale on which your grade point average (GPA) was registered. For example, include your GPA if it was 3.5 or higher on a 4.0 scale (3.5/4.0), or 5.0 and higher on a 6.0 scale (5.0/6.0).

If you graduated with honors, mention it in your degree listing, but leave out your GPA—listing both is redundant. If your class ranking would look more impressive than your GPA, use it.

Here are a few examples:

- *B.S., Computer Science, 1995, Tempe University, Tempe, Ariz. (3.8/4.0).*
- *Bachelor of Arts in Mass Communication, with honors, 1994, Boston University.*
- *Decatur High School, Decatur, Fla., 1995, ranked 4th in class of 300.*

Career changes

If you took some courses that aren't related to your degree but are specific to your new career goal, go ahead and profile them under your degree information.

For example, say, while finishing your degree in agricultural economics, you took several electives in political science. Now you're interested in pursuing a career as the legislative aid for a senator from a Corn Belt state.

Your listing would read:

- *B.S. Agricultural Economics, Iowa State University, Ames, Iowa (1993), 18 credit hours in political science.*

Internships, co-op work and foreign exchange experience

Definitely include any internships, whether for pay, class credit or volunteer experience. You'll probably want to include your internship accomplishments under the Experience heading, but you can decide that later. For now, just gather the information. Here's an example of how to do it:

- *B.S., Accounting, 1995, University of Delaware, Newark.*
- *One-semester audit internship at DuPont corporate headquarters, Wilmington, Del.*
- *Three-credit-hour internship in accounting for Registrar's Office, University of Delaware, Newark.*

Many students complete co-op work experiences while still in college. Again, your accomplishments may be best presented in the Experience section. However, if you decide to list it under Education (perhaps you've been in the work force for several years), follow the above example and substitute your co-op information. Your co-op experience shows you'll go that extra step to achieve your career goal.

Experiences as a foreign exchange student are also worth noting. Although they may not be related to your career goal, the fact that you studied abroad shows you enjoy a challenge and are willing to try new experiences.

Here's a sample listing:

- *B.A., Personnel Management, DePauw University, Greencastle, Ind. (1993).*
- *One year foreign study at Athens University in Athens, Greece.*

4. Licensing, certification and special skills/training

It's important to list any licenses or certifications to show the employer you're trained for the job, especially if you're in a skilled trade, such as an airline mechanic or a dental assistant.

While you'll be listing your qualifications and accomplishments under another heading, this section gives you the opportunity to indicate when you received your training and/or certification.

For professional licenses and certification, include:

- Name and type of license.
- State (or states) in which it is valid, if applicable.
- Date of certification.
- Number of the license, if appropriate.

Here are a few examples:

- *NALA Certified Legal Assistant, 1991.*
- *Virginia Teaching Certification, secondary education, 1990.*
- *Expanded Duties Dental Assistant Certification, 1995.*
- *Nevada Real Estate License, 1992.*

For special training, include the name of the course, where you took the course and the date you completed training.

For example:

- *Radiograph Certification, Indiana University School of Dentistry, Bloomington, Ind., May 1994.*
- *Certificate in Litigation and Trial Practice, The Paralegal Institute, Los Angeles, Calif., December 1993.*

You also might want to mention any on-the-job or special job-related training you've received, such as completing a computer course. You could state it as follows:

- *CAD software: 2-month training program, NASA Computer Training Center, Hampton, Va., September 1995.*

However, there's no need to list professional or personal development seminars, such as those that explain effective team-building techniques or how to enhance your self-esteem. No doubt you pick up valuable information, but simply completing the course isn't a particularly noteworthy accomplishment.

In this section, you'll also want to list any other special skills you might have, such as speaking a foreign language. Perhaps you know sign language. Or are a certified scuba instructor. If you're interested in a tourism job in the Caribbean, that special scuba skill could be a big selling point!

5. Military experience

Don't forget to profile your military experience, if you have any. Your special training and accomplishments are valuable, especially if they relate directly to your chosen civilian career. Be sure to list the following information for each tour of duty:

- Branch.
- Rank.
- Dates of service.
- Duties.
- Special skills learned.
- Accomplishments (include awards, citations, medals).

6. Memberships and activities

Here is your opportunity to list any memberships and activities you haven't already covered under Work Experience. Your activities don't necessarily have to be career-related, but if most of them are, you may want to consider using the heading Professional Affiliations.

In addition, if you have several professional and/or social memberships, don't try to include all of them. Just focus on the ones you think would show a benefit to an employer and those that are related to your career. Otherwise, list any community or civic activities and memberships you feel are important. As discussed earlier, employers are looking for "doers"—productive people. Your activities will show that you're a well-rounded person with interests outside of work. In addition, listing a few of your activities reflects your ability to manage a busy schedule.

One final note: Your listings in this section should be current and brief. Just include the name of the organizations and any leadership positions you hold.

Here are two examples:

- *Treasurer, Lion's Club.*
- *President, Board of Directors, Akron Community Theater.*

7. Awards and honors

For the most part, you've probably detailed any work-related awards or volunteer honors as accomplishments in the Work Experience or Volunteer Experience sections. However, if you've received an award that you think the employer will view as a benefit, list it here. Remember, though, that employers only take about 30 seconds to review your resume, and may never even get to this section.

If the honor is really important, you probably should move it to either the Work Experience or Volunteer Experience section where it's more likely to get noticed.

In summary

Well, that blank piece of paper isn't so blank anymore, is it? No doubt your experience and achievements seem more significant now that you've taken the time to gather them all together. This exercise is a great boost to the ego!

Before you move on, take time to review each section and make sure you've included every bit of applicable information. When you get ready to draft your resume, you may choose not to include all of it, but at least you have the option. In the next chapter, you'll learn to evaluate what should be included and how to best present it.

For now, go eat a hot fudge sundae or order that pizza. You've earned it! You're beyond intimidation, beyond that blank piece of paper and on your way to developing an effective resume.

Chapter 2

Making order of chaos

Now that you've gathered the information for your resume, no doubt you're itching to get started on the first draft.

But before you do, you'll need to consider how to organize and best present all that information. There are two basic formats to choose from.

Reviewing the following paragraphs will help you determine which format works best for you.

The chronological format

If you were to walk into any recruiter's office and rifle through the stack of resumes on his or her desk, most of them would be arranged in a chronological format.

The chronological format is the traditional format and, for the most part, is the format of choice. It organizes your employment history by date, beginning with your most recent position and working backwards. This format is a good choice if you've been in the job market for several years. For each position, you provide the following information:

- Employer's name and location.
- Dates of employment.
- Your position.
- Your responsibilities and accomplishments.

In a chronological format, information about your work experience typically makes up about 70 percent of the resume. This section usually appears after the job objective or skills summary. However, if your educational background is the most important qualification for the position you're seeking, you may want to put the education section first and then list your work experience. But we'll get into resume order at the end of the chapter.

You also can use this format to profile your volunteer experience. Just list volunteer positions the same way you would paid positions, including the name of the organization, the year of involvement, your position and your responsibilities and accomplishments.

In general, the chronological format identifies where you've been and what you've done to qualify you for the job. It works best when:

- You have a stable history of paid employment or volunteer work.
- You've worked in the same general field for several years and are pursuing employment in that area.
- You have advanced steadily throughout your career and can show an increase in level and responsibility.
- You have had few career changes and have spent a year or more in each of your jobs.

Employers tend to favor the chronological format because it's the one they're familiar with.

But what if you've gotten off to a bad start and haven't worked six months at any one job? Or you've stayed home a few years to raise children and now are ready to reenter the work force? Or you've recently graduated from school and have little or no job experience?

Then you need to consider a functional resume.

The functional format

If you don't have a stable work history, or if you've changed careers midstream, the functional resume may present your experience and accomplishments in the best light.

With a functional resume, your qualifications, experience and accomplishments are grouped together according to areas of skill, rather than tied to specific positions and dates. How you group your qualifications depends on your career direction, but possible headings for the groupings might be:

- Communication skills.
- Leadership skills.
- Customer service experience.
- Organizational skills.
- Technical experience.
- Instructional experience.
- Sales experience.

In a functional resume, emphasis is placed on what you've achieved and not where and when you achieved it. The idea is to highlight your skills in particular areas.

It's important to note that employers are not as familiar with the functional resume and tend to suspect that the prospective employee is trying to hide something. However, you should seriously consider the functional format if:

- Your work history doesn't exactly match your new career goals.
- You don't have a great deal of experience related to the position you're interested in.
- You have noticeable gaps in your work history.

Writing the rough draft

Okay. Now you're ready. Get out the notes and lists you made from Chapter 1 and grab that pencil or keyboard. It's time to start your rough draft. But before you dive in, remember these three essential factors:

- Put your best foot forward. Your resume is your yellow pages ad. Show how you can address a specific need—that you have the goods and can deliver. Emphasize the experience and qualifications that are most relevant to the position you're seeking. If you have more than one career goal, you'll need to create a different resume for each one and tailor each accordingly.

- Make every word count. Be clear and concise. Your resume will probably get only 30 seconds of attention, so focus on the information that best details your qualifications.

- It's just a rough draft. No need for perfection at this point. Just pay attention to content. There will be time for polishing later.

Length, words and punctuation

While you don't need to worry about too much polish at this point, you do need to consider length. Your resume should be no longer than two pages. Employers won't read any more than that, anyway. If you can fit your resume onto one page, that's fine—don't stretch it to two thinking it will appear more impressive. Employers are looking for, among other qualities, strong organizational and communication skills. If you can't sum up your qualifications in two pages or less, they'll pass you by.

As discussed in Chapter 1, use words with a "punch"—action words that carry an impact. For help, see the sample list of such words on the following page.

Use those action words to begin tightly written phrases—your entries don't need to be full sentences. In fact, it's best if they're not—it keeps you from getting wordy.

Action words

Use any of the following action words to add "punch" and energy to your resume:

accomplished	enlarged	prepared
achieved	established	presided
adjusted	evaluated	processed
administered	examined	produced
advised	expanded	programmed
analyzed	formulated	promoted
approved	founded	proposed
arranged	flagged	provided
assisted	gathered	purchased
budgeted	generated	recommended
built	guided	reduced
calculated	headed	referred
charted	identified	regulated
compared	implemented	reorganized
compiled	improved	replaced
completed	increased	reported
composed	initiated	represented
conducted	inspected	researched
consolidated	installed	restored
constructed	instituted	reviewed
consulted	instructed	revised
controlled	interpreted	scheduled
conceptualized	invented	selected
coordinated	justified	served
counseled	lectured	sold
created	led	solved
decreased	lobbied	studied
delivered	maintained	supervised
designated	managed	supplied
designed	modified	systematized
detected	motivated	taught
determined	negotiated	tested
developed	obtained	traced
devised	operated	trained
diagnosed	organized	translated
directed	ordered	updated
discovered	overhauled	utilized
distributed	performed	won
edited	persuaded	wrote
eliminated	planned	

Leave out unnecessary articles, such as "I," "an" and "the."

And finally, don't get too hung up on punctuation. The most important factor is to be consistent throughout your resume.

Whether you list the dates as "October, 1994" or "October 1994" isn't all that critical—just be consistent.

The chronological resume

Typically, a chronological resume is organized in the following order:

1. Name header.
2. Objective (optional).
3. Summary of skills/qualifications (optional).
4. Work experience.
5. Education.
6. Memberships/activities/honors (optional).

Name header

The name header, which tells employers who you are and how to reach you, is always at the top of your resume. If you want to make it especially noticeable, set the header—or just your name—in bold face.

Include your full name (first and last names and middle initial), your street address and phone number. If you are a college student with a temporary campus address (or for some other reason have a temporary address), list temporary and future addresses, phone numbers and dates you can be reached at each address.

If you feel comfortable receiving calls at work, list your work phone number. If not, use your home number and make sure an answering machine or voice-mail service is ready to capture any and every call. Prospective employers will call during business hours, the same time you'll be working. So make sure you don't miss their calls.

If you decide to use an answering machine, record a professional outgoing message and state your full name so employers know they've reached the right number. Otherwise, they may not leave a message. Return any calls immediately.

Objective (optional)

You don't have to use a job objective. After all, a good resume tells employers what they want, not what *you* want. If you decide to use an objective, put it right under the name header and use a heading, such as Objective, Job Objective or Career Objective.

State exactly the type of position you want in 12 words or less. Show the employer you're focused on your career goal.

For example, the following objective only wastes space and doesn't tell the employer anything:

To apply my experience and knowledge, enhance my management skills and develop professionally with a growth-oriented company.

How does that set you apart from the hundreds of others seeking the same position? Instead, try this:

A computer programmer for an aeronautics firm.

A product account manager for a dental products distributor.

The above two examples give the employer a much better impression of what you want to do.

Summary of qualifications/skills (optional)

The skills summary, although optional, provides an excellent opportunity for you to briefly summarize your qualifications and convince the employer to read the rest of your resume. The summary should be targeted to your job goal and highlight specific experience, skills and training related to the position you're seeking.

Place your summary immediately after the name header or objective (if you use one) and call it Skills Summary, Summary of Qualifications or Experience Summary. It can be in paragraph or "bullet" form. If you decide to use a paragraph, keep it to two or three shorts sentences, as in the following example:

Award-winning graphic artist with five years experience with state-of-the-art technologies on IBM and Macintosh systems. Also skilled in video production and computer-generated images. Software knowledge includes Adobe Photoshop, Aldus Freehand, Adobe Premier and Aldus PageMaker.

If you decide on a "bulleted" format, list four or five points, such as:

- *10 years legal experience in products liability, medical malpractice, contracts, real estate and personal injury litigation.*
- *Trained and experienced in photography and in investigation and interviewing techniques.*
- *Strong computer skills, including detailed knowledge of WordPerfect 5.1 and Page Maker.*
- *NALA certified.*

Sometimes it's more productive to complete your resume, determine your strong points and then go back and write your summary of qualifications. However you choose to handle your skills summary, remember to always put your most important and most relevant qualifications first.

Experience

The Experience section of your resume will most likely take up the biggest chunk of space, and is the section most employers are interested in. Remember, in most chronological formats, this section makes up 70 percent of the resume.

You have a couple of options here, depending on your situation. This section isn't necessarily just for paid work experience. It's a great place to include your volunteer work.

Here are some suggestions on how to list your experience:

1. **List paid and volunteer positions separately.** For paid positions, use headings such as Employment History or Professional Experience. Use Volunteer Experience, Related Experience or Other Experience for your volunteer positions. Place one section immediately after the other. Your order will depend on which shows the strongest qualifications for your job goal.

2. **Combine volunteer and paid positions.** Combining your volunteer and paid experiences can be quite effective, especially when both experiences are targeted toward your job goal, or when the combination blends two experiences toward one career goal. Use either Experience or Professional and Volunteer Experience for your heading.

   You may, however, decide not to combine the two experiences if you've held paid and volunteer positions at the same time. Trying to list them all together on one time line could make it difficult for the employer to sort out. Also, if your volunteer work is quite different from your paid experience and isn't all that relevant to your career goal, you might be better off listing the experiences separately.

3. **List paid positions only.** If your volunteer experience isn't all that extensive or relevant to your job goal, you're better off just listing your activities at the end of the resume in the memberships and activities section.

   The listing for your positions in the experience section should look something like this:

1993-current   Operations Assistant, Replay Records, Indianapolis, Ind.
- *Assist in managing and supervising central warehouse operations, including traffic management and distribution.*
- *Contract, coordinate and schedule freight operations between four stores.*
- *Recommended and implemented new handling procedure, which better protects fragile warehouse inventory.*
- *Assisted in reorganizing warehouse operations and freight distribution, resulting in $75,000 savings annually.*

If you've held several jobs with one company, draw attention to it. Such staying power shows you're a loyal, promotable employee. To avoid repeating the employer's name for each position, and to show your ability to handle increased responsibility, you might want to list your positions as shown in the example below.

1987-present, Haverford Barge Company, Cincinnati, Ohio

Director, 1993-present.
Handle profit/loss for $1.5M export facility. Provide general terminal services sales for 12 Midwest river facilities.

- Manage daily merchandising and personnel for Ohio export facility, which has achieved gross sales of more than $40M in last two years, a 45% increase.
- Expanded business by developing new European customers in Spain, France and Portugal.
- Manage all risk aspects for commodities and negotiate all freight and FOE arrangements.

Sales/Special Projects Manager, 1990-1993.
Coordinated all sales work for products other than whole grain at largest river facility.

- Completed contracts with ocean freight companies for bagging contracts and took program to more than 40,000 short tons in one year.
- Developed and directed small fleet of owner/operators to expand business and take advantage of various seasonal trucking opportunities.

Grain Merchandiser, 1985-1990.
One of two merchandisers responsible for originating grain on an FOE truck basis in four states.

- Expanded services by establishing truck line and exceeded all first-year forecasts by $.5M.

In a chronological format, list your most recent position first and then work backwards. Usually, your first few entries will contain more information than the last few, indicating more extensive experience as you've progressed through your career.

When listing your positions, be sure to include:

- Name of employer.
- Employer's location.
- Your dates of employment (or affiliation, if volunteer work).
- Your position or job title.
- A summary of your responsibilities.
- Your major accomplishments.

You'll want to provide all of this information for the first four to six positions on your resume, or for your first seven to 10 years of experience. For any remaining positions, go into detail only if you have a particular achievement to highlight. Otherwise, just list the employer's name and location, your position and your dates of employment.

Here's a good way to present the elements for each position:

- **Employer or organization name and location.** List the company's full name and location. If the organization is known by a nickname or acronym, use the full name and then follow with the acronym in parentheses. For example: Abbott Lane Pharmaceuticals (ALP). After that first reference, you may use the initials.

- **Dates of employment.** State the month and year you began and left each position. If you've been in the work force several years and have held each position a year or more, you can omit the months.

- **Your job title.** The best advice in this area? Don't embellish. Avoid trying to improve your job status by enhancing your job title. Attempting to look better to a prospective employer could get you caught in what might be perceived as a lie. Your job responsibilities and accomplishments, which immediately follow the job title, best tell your story. Don't try to do it with creative job titles.

  However, if your company uses unusual job titles, such as "group leader" for the more commonly understood "supervisor," it would be okay to list "supervisor" on your resume. You might mention it to your former boss so he or she is aware what you've done and won't be surprised if contacted as a reference.

- **Summary of responsibilities.** Keep it brief, preferably to one or two succinct statements. Use broad terms to indicate your level of responsibility and focus on aspects most relevant to the position you're seeking. There's no need to explain to a dental sales company what a dental sales representative does. And don't forget your "action" words!

- **Major accomplishments.** Here's your chance to show the employer you were successful in your position. State your accomplishments, if possible, in quantitative terms: how much money you saved the company annually or the percentage you increased sales. Be specific and, again, use action words. If you're having trouble, refer back to Chapter 1, where developing this section is discussed in length.

Education

Information about your education generally follows the experience section. However, your educational background should come before your experience if:

- You're a recent college graduate with little job experience.
- You're changing careers and your education is more relevant to your new career than your recent job experience.
- You're seeking a job for which specialized education is a prerequisite for employment.

The education section contains only basic information, including the name and location of the school, date of graduation, degree or major area of study and GPA (optional).

List only your most recent degree, unless you want to list both your bachelor's and your master's degrees (they may be in different areas, such as a bachelor's degree in management and a master's degree in marketing). If you have a college degree, employers assume you graduated from high school, so omit that high school listing and use the space for more important information that sells you and your qualifications.

When stating college and trade-school degrees, you can use abbreviations (B.S., B.A., M.B.A.) or spell them out (Bachelor of Arts). It doesn't matter—just be consistent.

If you want to emphasize your degree, put it first in the entry, followed by the school information, like this:

Bachelor of Science in Computer Science, 1993,
Eastern Montana University, Elkville

Note that because the state's name is in the university's name, there's no need to repeat the state name. Only the city is listed.

If you graduated from a well-known and well-respected college, you may want to put the college first instead, like this:

Harvard University, Cambridge, Mass., B.S. in Business Management, Cum Laude, 1995

For guidance on special issues, such as if you didn't graduate from college, had a less-than-spectacular GPA or are changing careers, refer back to Chapter 1.

High school education—to include or not to include? List your high school education only if you are a recent graduate or did not attend college or trade school. If you earned a GED, list when and where you received it. A typical high school listing would look like this:

Carthidge High School, Carthidge, Wisconsin, graduated May 1989

If you attended more than one high school, list only the one from which you received your diploma.

You might consider listing a few school courses if they're relevant to the job you're seeking and you have no job experience. But don't get carried away—list just a few.

If you've been out of high school several years, there's really no need to list your high school information. By now, you've probably got some solid job experience, and that will interest an employer much more than your high school education. So just leave it off.

Licensing, certification and special skills/training

After you detail your education, you'll need to relate any special training or licensing. If you'd rather, you can include this information in the education section.

Indicate any special training you've had and any professional licenses or certification you possess. Your heading will vary depending on the information included. Some suggestions: Professional Licenses, Certification or Special Training.

Remember to include:

- Name and type of license.
- State or states in which it is valid.
- Date license/certification acquired.
- Number of license, if appropriate.

Military experience

Don't forget to profile your military experience, including special training and accomplishments. Developing this information is covered in Chapter 1.

Memberships and activities

One of the last sections on your resume should cover your outside interests. Your activities don't necessarily have to be related to your career goal, although it helps if they are. They simply show employers that you can manage your time well and enjoy a few outside activities. Again, the title you give this section should communicate its content, such as Professional Affiliations, Community Activities or Memberships and Activities. If you belong to several organizations or have several outside activities, list only those you feel will mean the most to prospective employers.

Awards and honors

If you've received any special recognition related to your work, you should mention that honor in your experience section. However, if you have some other award or honor that you think would be meaningful to the employer, list it here. Just remember, the hiring manager may never get to this part of your resume, so don't expect to "wow" him or her here—do it earlier!

The functional resume

Most elements of the functional resume are handled in the same manner as a chronological resume, except for work experience and accomplishments.

Instead of listing each position you've held on a detailed time line, you'll profile your experience and accomplishments according to areas of skill.

The order for a functional resume is as follows:

1. Name header.
2. Objective (optional, but suggested if not using skills summary).
3. Summary of skills/qualifications (optional, but suggested if not using job objective).
4. Skills/achievements profile.
5. Education.

Objective and Summary of skills

Employers may have trouble determining your career or job goal from a functional resume, so it's a good idea to include a Job Objective or Skills Summary.

Present your information as you would if writing a chronological resume (see that section earlier in this chapter).

Skill and experience profile

Divide your experience into general areas of skill, such as management skills, communication skills or sales skills, and briefly state experience, qualifications and accomplishments related to each area.

To determine which skill areas to highlight, consider what the prospective employer needs for the position you're seeking. Your experience can come from paid positions, volunteer work or in-the-home responsibilities, such as budgeting the household income.

Under each skills heading, list four or five experiences or accomplishments. The sample below profiles a woman with no paid job experience who's seeking a position as a food service manager. Note how she has selected skills categories relevant to such a position (management skills, budgeting skills) and has strong volunteer and in-home experience to support her qualifications.

Organizational/management skills

- For 10 years, organized, hosted, planned menu and supervised preparation of all food for 300 guests at annual cattle association picnic.
- Organize up to 120 volunteers and supervise food service and forecasting for State Fair beef tent, raising $100,000 annually for state association.
- Chair meal portion of home economics club's annual fall bazaar/ luncheon, including purchasing goods and supervising food preparation.
- Organize and supervise up to 25 volunteers for sorority's annual fall craft sale.

Financial budgeting skills

- Skilled in handling computerized bookkeeping for 1,200-acre grain and 250-head cattle farming operation.
- Initiated and completed data entry from manual to computerized record keeping system, reducing bookkeeping time and improving account analysis.
- Experienced in monthly business and household budgeting and timely payment of personal and business accounts.
- Consistently bring food purchases in under budget and increase net gain for a variety of organizations.

Special dietary experience

- Experienced in planning and creating low-fat, low-sugar and low-sodium meals.
- Skilled in presenting knowledgeable instruction on proper food handling and storage.

Using a time line

While other resume books say it's not necessary to include specific dates for your employment or volunteer experience in a functional resume, omitting such information may make prospective employers suspicious. They may feel you're trying to hide something.

Your entries can be brief, but you're smart to include them. Present them in chronological order, such as the following:

Work history

- Assistant farm manager and bookkeeper, Raleigh, Ohio, 1985-present.

- President, Raleigh County Home Economics Club, Raleigh, Ohio, 1990-current.

- Food manager, Ohio Cattle Association, Columbus, Ohio, 1985-1995.

Other elements

All other elements of the resume follow the guidelines established in the chronological format section of this chapter.

Things to remember

As you work on your resume, remember these three key tips:

- **Action words.** Don't use wishy-washy, vague terms. Give your resume power with action words (see page 22).

- **Achievements and accomplishments.** Make sure your resume isn't a giant job description, but rather a tightly written history of your job experiences and *accomplishments*.

- **Simple language.** Forget the showy, flowery or creative approach. Impress employers with your ability to communicate clearly and effectively with simple language in concise phrases.

Things to forget

You may have noticed there's been no discussion about photos, personal statistics or job references. That's because they don't belong on a resume. Here are some other elements that are best left off of your resume:

The heading "RESUME." Employers know a resume when they see one. Don't waste space by stating the obvious.

Job references. Almost anyone can provide a reference. The fact that you have a few doesn't distinguish you from the crowd. Wait until the employer asks for references before you provide them.

However, if you know someone who is well-known or respected by the employer, and that person has agreed to provide you with a reference, you could attach a separate sheet with that person's address and phone number. Make sure those on your list are aware they may receive a phone call.

Salary information. Providing salary information allows a prospective employer to eliminate you from consideration (you're too expensive) or determine how little he or she can get away with paying you. Don't include it on your resume.

A better way to address the situation is to mention in your cover letter that you will be happy to discuss your salary requirements when you have a better idea of what the job entails. But make mention of this issue only if the prospective employer mentions it first!

Personal statistics. Details of your personal life aren't important to your ability to perform the job, so leave them out. What does the fact that you're 6'4" and married have to do with managing a record store? It's considered unprofessional to include such information.

Photos. Again, maintain a professional image. Don't include a photo. Many employers, to avoid potential discrimination, will remove the picture before circulating the resume, anyway.

Personality profiles. Hiring professionals agree that statements such as "hard working," "team player" and "dedicated" are ignored because they are biased. So leave out your personal attributes and let your experience show that you're "hard working," "a team player" and "dedicated."

Testimonials. Testimonials—endorsements written by former employers—don't belong on a resume. Let your accomplishments and experience speak for themselves. If you have a testimonial on the writer's company letterhead, you can attach it to your resume, if you wish. Just realize it could be construed as biased and overlooked.

Remember, you're only working on a rough draft of your resume, so don't demand perfection just yet. Mull things over, make changes, and when you think you're ready to move on, read Chapter 3 to learn how to design your resume with the "read me" look!

Chapter 3

Designing with the "read me" look

Think back to Ted's Tire Service ad. What made you look at the ad in the first place? Wasn't it because it had a nice, neat and clean look? That there was plenty of white space? And that the type size was adequate—not so small that your eyes had to strain to pick out some bit of important information?

Now, imagine your resume sitting on a hiring manager's desk. Have you made it inviting to look at, with lots of white space, a neat and clean appearance and an easy-to-read typeface?

Bingo! First impressions are important. You may have achieved 250 percent of your sales goal for a Fortune 500 company, but if your information is poorly presented, no one's going to give it a second glance.

And since you've gone to an awful lot of time and trouble to carefully organize your information, select an appropriate format and anguish over effective wording, you sure don't want to reach "file 13" because of lousy presentation.

Want to make a good first impression? Looking for a professional presentation? Your strategy is simple:

- Make it easy to read.
- Use lots of white space.
- Make it neat.
- Make it clean.

In addition, although you won't have "RESUME" tattooed across the top of the page, your product should look like a resume. Several job hunters have come up with clever ideas that get noticed for their creativeness...and nothing else. Gimmicks rarely work. When preparing your resume, it's best to be businesslike and professional.

Granted, some job seekers in creative fields have been successful with a nontraditional approach, but more often than not, the idea fails.

So, how do you make a good first impression with your resume? Try these 20 tips:

20 tips to a great-looking resume

1. **Limit your resume to one or two pages.** Previously, everyone believed resumes should be only one page. Today, two-page resumes are quite acceptable. It's understood that if you've been working for several years, you may need two pages to fully document your experience and accomplishments. Don't cut out vital information just to get your resume down to one page. And never go more than two pages.

2. **Don't cram three pages of information onto two.** If pages are too full, you need to do a little editing and focus on information that's most relevant to your chosen field. Reducing type size, shrinking margins and closing up spaces isn't the way to do it. A crowded look can be overwhelming and uninviting.

3. **If you have a two-page resume, add "continued" at the bottom of the first page,** and put your name and "page 2" at the top of the second page. If your two pages become separated, they're easily identified and brought back together.

4. **Use a serif typeface**—the kind with the little "doodads" on all the letters. For example, this book uses the serif typeface New Century Schoolbook. Tests have proven serif type is easier on the eye...and therefore, easier to read. Other serif typefaces include Palatino, Bookman, Times, Courier and Souvenir.

   This typeface is Helvetica. It's a sans serif style. Don't use it.

5. **Stick to traditional typefaces.** Now that home personal computers are much more affordable and desktop publishing software is readily available, job seekers have a veritable treasure trove of typefaces to chose from. But again, let professionalism rule out. Stay away from the fancy or cutesy types, and stick with Times, Bookman, Palatino or Souvenir.

6. **Select a readable size.** Never use anything smaller than 10-point type for the body of your resume. You may go up to 12 points. Your header can be even larger—typically one or two points higher than your body type.

7. **Don't mix type faces.** Resist the urge to play with typefaces. Pick one and stick with it.

8. **Highlight with boldface type.** Boldface type is the darker, heavier type that leads off each of the entries on this page. Using boldface type can help you emphasize certain elements of your resume and draw attention to them.

For example, you might want to boldface your name, job titles, the names of employers and your degree. These elements would then stand out as a recruiter glances over your resume. However, don't get too carried away, or you'll lose the effect.

9. **Use all-caps and underlining for section heads only,** and even then, sparingly. Don't underline words or phrases in your body copy. Research shows that underlining and capitalizing whole words slows and even stops the eye while reading. Save these treatments for your name header and section heads.

10. **Avoid italic type.** Italic type often is used in publications to emphasize a word or phrase, but don't do it in your body copy. First of all, it just adds another type style, which is something you want to avoid. In addition, your goal in writing your resume is to emphasize everything through clear, concise phrases. Italics would only be redundant and could actually detract, as italic type is harder to read.

11. **Use generous margins.** Leave at least a one-inch margin at the top of the page and, if possible, one-inch borders on the other three sides. Never use any less than a half-inch border. Wide margins create a pleasant, uncluttered look.

12. **Use "ragged right" layout.** Don't worry about "justifying" or "evening" your right margin, such as the right margins in this book. (Notice how all of the lines end at exactly the same point.) Instead, just let the lines end where they may, as in the following example:

   This paragraph uses a ragged right style. Notice how the uneven line breaks create attractive white space around the edges. A justified paragraph looks "boxy" and places needed white space between words instead of at the end of the lines.

13. **Avoid hyphens.** Hyphens break up words and, consequently, the flow of a hiring manager's eyes as he or she reads about your qualifications. By avoiding hyphens, reading is uninterrupted and, as discussed in #12, you maintain a wide right margin with lots of white space.

14. **Single-space between lines of each listing.** And double-space between sections and paragraphs. This approach breaks up body copy and creates an attractive, balanced look.

15. **Use bullets to highlight accomplishments.** Key points can get lost in a paragraph format. Using bullets helps organize information in digestible pieces and works to emphasize those key points. Look at the following examples—you'll notice the difference immediately.

Military Personnel Management Officer, Arizona Air National Guard, Midway Field, Ariz. Administered and managed personnel function for staff of 26. Increased office support capabilities and decreased required overtime by 50%. Initiated new mail procedures and streamlined and standardized routing forms and procedures, which improved work flow and reduced "lag" time. As central coordinator for Headquarters' enlisted members, designed programs which led to documented increase in performance, production and morale.

Military Personnel Management Officer, Arizona Air National Guard, Midway Field, Ariz. Administered and managed personnel function for staff of 26.

- Increased office support capabilities and decreased required overtime by 50%.
- Initiated new mail procedures and streamlined and standardized routing forms and procedures, which improved work flow and reduced "lag" time.
- As central coordinator for headquarters' enlisted members, designed programs which led to documented increase in performance, production and morale.

16. **Keep bulleted items to two or three lines of copy.** The whole idea of using bullets is to provide information in short bursts. When you start getting windy, bullets lose their effect.

17. **Keep paragraph length to no more than four or five lines.** Otherwise your reader will give up trying to wade through the sea of information.

18. **Use a short line length.** Studies have shown the easiest copy to read is that which asks your eyes to travel just a short distance back and forth across the page. To keep your line length short, indent all body copy about two inches from the left margin and put only section heads and accompanying dates to the left. You can find several sample resumes that effectively use this format at the end of this book.

19. **Keep it simple.** Don't try to combine three or four different design styles into one resume. Just pick one style and use it. Your qualifications are the most important part of your resume. The design just encourages others to read it.

20. **Find the look that fits you.** At the end of this book are sample resumes in a variety of styles. Find one you like, modify it if necessary...and create the resume that reflects you.

Editing your resume

Now that you've roughed out your resume, have it in some semblance of order and have applied the 20 tips to a great looking resume, it's time to put it on the chopping block and trim off that excess fat.

What? You think it's pretty good? Well, maybe it is. But it never hurts to do a little fine tuning. Remember, you want a professional product, one that shows you've spent time and thoughtful consideration putting it together. You've got to be sure you've communicated your value and worth in an effective, attractive format. If getting the job is important, then so should be editing your resume. Basically, you need to look at three areas:

- The big picture (overall effect).
- The little picture (details).
- The proofing (typos and grammar).

The big picture

When you first started organizing your information for your resume, you determined what should be included and what shouldn't. Well, it's time to do it again. Here are some questions to ask yourself as you look over your almost-finished product:

Have I shown I can fill a need? Your resume should not be a lengthy job description. Have you told the employer what you can do for him or her? Have you communicated your worth and benefit through results-oriented accomplishments? Have you detailed your achievements? If not, get busy and start listing your specific accomplishments.

Have I chosen the right format? Whether you've selected a chronological or functional format, make sure you've highlighted your strengths and haven't raised questions. Does your functional format look like you're trying to hide something? Does your chronological format make you look like a job-hopper?

Is my resume too long or too cluttered? Stand back. Hold your resume up. Is it jam-packed full of words and lines? Have you left adequate margins? Is your resume longer than two pages? Then, trim that fat. Your result will be a tighter-written, more attractive, more effective resume.

Does every element count? If you used a job objective, is it meaningful and targeted, or just a vague group of words that says little about you and what you want? Does your skills summary include experience specifically related to your chosen job or career? Do all those memberships you listed really mean anything to an employer? If not, eliminate them. Don't waste valuable space on elements that don't communicate your value or accomplishments.

This would be a good time to show your resume to friends, family or co-workers to see what suggestions they might have. They'll be much more objective and might even come up with a few skills or achievements you missed.

The little picture

Once you've asked yourself those "big picture" questions and feel you've sufficiently addressed them, it's time to examine the details.

Here's a checklist to guide you through the process:

❑ **Name header**
Is it at the top of the page?
Did you use the most professional sounding form of your name (no nicknames)?
Is your address correct? Have you included dates with your temporary and permanent address information?
Did you list a phone number where you can be reached easily or where a message can be left?
Did you include an area code? Did you transpose any numbers?

❑ **Job objective**
Is your job objective focused and precise?
Is it stated in 12 words or less?
Does your experience relate to your objective?
Does it exclude you from other positions you might be interested in? If so, omit it.

❑ **Skills summary**
Is it targeted to the job you're seeking? Does it highlight the qualifications and experience that are most important to your prospective employer?
Is it short and concise (two or three brief sentences or four or five bulleted points)? Have you placed your most relevant qualifications first?

❑ **Experience profile: Chronological format**
Did you include the correct starting and ending dates (month and year) for each position?
Did you use your correct job title or a revised title that accurately reflects your responsibilities and duties? Did you include the correct name and location of your employers?
Did you limit your job descriptions to short sentences?
Are any paragraphs longer than five lines? Any bulleted items longer than three lines?

❏ **Experience profile: Functional format**

Did you use skills categories most relevant to the job you want?

Did you use business-like terms for skills category headings (management, organizational, sales, etc.)?

Did you include a brief chronological listing of your work experience at the end of your resume?

❏ **Experience profile: All formats**

Did you use strong action words to describe your contributions and achievements?

Did you eliminate "I," "the" and "an" from your body copy?

Did you use acronyms, initials or unfamiliar terms that might not be understood by the reader?

Did you repeat words, especially action words? Change a few of them. Did you quantify your accomplishments rather than just describe them? For example, did you talk about the money you saved or the percentage you increased sales?

If you listed an award, did you explain why you were honored? Did you use the correct name and date for the award?

❏ **Education**

Did you check and correctly state the dates you earned your degree or attended school?

Did you verify the type of degree earned and list the correct location of the school from which you earned it?

Did you verify data related to certifications, licenses and other training?

❏ **Other**

Did you include personal references? Pictures? Salary information? Personality traits? The heading "RESUME?" Omit them!

❏ **Great looks**

Did you leave a one-inch margin at the top and no less than half-inch borders on all other sides?

Did you use at least a 10-point type size?

Did you use a serif type face? Did you use boldface type effectively?

Did you use a ragged-right margin?

Did you break up blocks of copy with line spacing?

Did you use bullets to emphasize specific points within listings?

If your resume is two pages, did you put "continued" at the bottom of the first page, and your name and "page 2" at the top of the second page?

Are you consistent with spacing, headline treatment, listing treatment, etc., throughout your resume?

The proofing

Getting a little trying, isn't it? This editing process may be tedious, but it's essential to an effective resume. Go ahead and take a break. And not just an hour. Take a whole day. No doubt by now your eyes are crossed and bulging. Or maybe you're afraid you're going to have to call that hair replacement service before this little exercise is complete.

Well, don't do yourself in. But when you're ready to move on, you'll be ready for the final proofreading.

You've put so much effort into your resume at this point. Don't take the chance of having it tossed out by a prospective employer because you spelled "achieved" wrong or used "1938" instead of "1983." Here are some tips to help you pick out those errors:

- If you're working on a computer, use your spell-check program to catch misspelled words. It won't, however, find misused words, such as *you're* instead of *your*. You'll have to detect those yourself.

- Read your resume out loud. It will help you find typos and misspelled words, awkward sentence structure and repetitive words.

- Read backwards. Start in the lower right-hand corner and move toward the top of the page. This slows you down and makes you look at each word individually.

- Ask for help. Get several people to look over your resume. The more eyes, the better.

In other sections of the book you've been admonished for striving for perfection. Well, *now* is the time. Don't give in until you're sure your resume is perfect.

A few production tips

Again, now that you've come this far, don't skimp on looks. If you don't have a home personal computer, type your resume on an office-quality typewriter or hire a professional word processor to type it for you.

If you hire a word processor, have him or her provide you with a copy of your resume on a computer disk. When you need to update your resume, you can take the disk back or—if he or she no longer provides typing services—to another typist with the same word processing system.

Many print shops also offer desktop publishing and typesetting services, but you'll want to investigate prices first. If the shop offers only typesetting services, updating your resume could be costly.

If the business has a desktop publishing service, be sure to ask how long they maintain files and how they charge for revisions. Ask if they'll give you your resume on a computer disk for a slight additional charge. With the proliferation of desktop publishing services, you're bound to be able to find someone to help you with updates as long as you have your resume on a computer disk.

Here are a few other considerations:

• Avoid copy machines. They just don't provide the quality you're looking for. You'll inevitably end up with smudges, streaks and lines. You're better off to use a print shop and get quality results.

• Select white, off-white, ivory or buff colored paper. And use only black ink. This combination provides excellent contrast and ensures easy readability.

• Choose a good-quality, medium weight paper, preferably 24-pound stock.

• Select a paper stock with a conservative finish. Texture is okay as long as it doesn't take over as the main focus of your resume, cause the ink to crack or decrease readability.

• Make sure matching stationery (for your cover letters) and envelopes are available to complete your professional look.

Some final thoughts

Your resume isn't cast in stone. Actually, it's a fairly flexible body of work that changes and grows with you.

So keep it current. As soon as you get a new job, earn a degree, complete special training or achieve a significant goal, get it on your resume.

You never know what tomorrow may bring. Someone in your network may call and tell you your dream job is open at KLM Company. The position isn't being publicized, they're hiring soon and you need to get your resume over there right away. If you have to rework your resume, have a typist make corrections and dash it off it to the print shop before you can send it out, you'll lose valuable time...and maybe a chance to interview for your dream job.

In addition, there are no guarantees in today's job market. Many companies are "right sizing." Reorganizations abound. It's best to adopt the wise scout motto: "Always be prepared."

Your personal life may suddenly change, too. Suppose your spouse is laid off, and you need to go back to work? Or some unforeseen, long-term medical expenses arise and your family needs a second income immediately. During such a stressful time, the last thing you need to be dealing with is writing your resume. Wouldn't it be a relief to know you could go right to your file cabinet and pull out a professional-looking, current resume that effectively communicates your qualifications and achievements? Don't wait!

The remainder of this book includes 101 sample resumes, which cover various personal situations and careers. The resumes are arranged in a variety of formats and are preceded by brief paragraphs that emphasize the strong points in the resumes.

Because this book is not standard paper size (8½" x 11"), all of the resumes have been reduced to fit the book's page size. Please note margins for resumes in this book may not necessarily be one-inch, and typefaces may not be 10-point. However, you still should follow the guidelines established in this chapter under the section "20 tips to a great-looking resume."

Part 2

101 great resumes

Now, we're getting into the heart of the book!

Following are 101 resumes depicting all sorts of situations and specific occupations. Beginning on page 60 are 37 resumes that illustrate life situations, from seeking a job right after high school to diving back into the work force after raising a family. Then, starting on page 114, the 64 resumes that follow represent a variety of occupations, from accounting to writing.

Remember, that there is no *one right way* to structure a resume, nor should you try to pick up an exact resume from this book and drop in your own personal information, cookie-cutter style. Review the comments about the resumes on the following pages, examine the resumes themselves—and with what you've learned from Part I, you should have the tools and knowledge to create your own great job-winning resume!

Situational resumes

Recent high school graduate   60
with job experience

Paid work experience and leadership roles in school organizations are reflected in Christopher's well-balanced resume. Note how his functional resume emphasizes the skills and abilities he's developed through work and school activities. He quantifies results where possible and communicates his value as a responsible individual who could succeed in a variety of entry-level positions.

Recent high school graduate   61
with no paid job experience

Judy doesn't have any paid job experience, but her classwork, volunteer work and vocational accomplishments reflect her capabilities. She chose to write a functional resume to successfully highlight her career-related skills. Because she has no paid work experience, Judy decided to include some relevant course work and the fact that she studied a vocational curriculum. Notice she rounds off her resume by mentioning memberships and awards affiliated with her chosen position.

Recent college graduate with job experience   62-64

Janet has demonstrated her ability to communicate by presenting a clear and concise resume. Her work history lends itself well to a chronological resume and gives her the opportunity to highlight her career-related achievements and contributions. Her GPA and campus activities only strengthen an already impressive resume. Notice that her honors and accomplishments are directly related to her chosen field.

Michelle has some job experience, but her education and high GPA are her strong points, so she places her education first. She has a specific veterinary interest, which she covers in a short, clear objective. Note that all of her work experience supports her career goal.

Recent college graduate with no paid job experience   65

Terry may not have any paid job experience, but his campus activities and accomplishments show just how valuable an employee he would be. His functional resume communicates his management and sales achievements and leadership abilities. He includes an objective because his career goal may not be evident from his skills and abilities profile. Note Terry lists his positions with the newspaper and fraternity house as experience, even though they were nonpaid positions.

Earned college degree mid-career   66-67

After nearly 10 years of changing diapers and wiping runny noses, Bridgette is ready for a change. While her day-care center is quite successful, she wants something more. So she has gone to school and earned an elementary education degree and teaching license. Although she has some instructional background and extensive experience as a day-care director, her education is her strong point, and she lists it first. Her career-related volunteer work and additional activities show she's a well-rounded individual who enjoys working with children. As with all beginning teachers, she includes a license-specific objective and student teaching experience.

Earned advanced degree mid-career   68

Lori is an accomplished accountant, but in the last few years she has developed an interest in sales and marketing. She decided to pursue a position as an account manager with her current employer and found she's good at it. To enhance her marketability, she has earned an MBA in marketing. Lori does an excellent job quantifying her sales achievements and emphasizing her strong customer relations skills and "go-getter" attitude.

Strong education, weak experience 69

After eight years in school, Emilio now has his doctorate degree, but little work experience to support it. Therefore, he lists his education first—including his dissertation topics—to provide employers with more information about his knowledge, achievements and areas of specialty. He highlights the fact that his theses were published—a noteworthy accomplishment. Although his work experience is limited, it's solid, career-related and covers specific achievements.

Strong experience, weak education 70-71

James never earned a college degree. He took a job as a machinist to help pay for his education...and never left the work place. James now holds a management position, and, as a result, offers prospective employers solid experience and proven ability to assume increased responsibilities. Note how James quantifies his achievements and high quality standards. He profiles his skills and strong work history first and includes his limited education at the end of his resume.

Seeking career change 72-75

If you're pursuing a career change, make sure you don't confuse prospective employers by including irrelevant information first. Note that each of these career changers lists a clear objective and includes a profile highlighting skills relevant to her *new* career goal.

Martin has been in the financial area and has some noteworthy accomplishments. But he's gone back to school, earned his education degree and is ready to get started as a music teacher. His solid background as a tutor, piano instructor and choral director support his career change, so he lists them first. He includes his other employment history, even though it is not career-related, to show he's a dependable and employable individual. Since Martin mentions his degree in his skills summary, he saves his education listing for last.

Melinda has always had an interest in designing homes, but a growing family and other demands left little time or funds for additional education. Now that her load has lifted, she's decided to pursue a career change. She lists her strongest points—education and awards—first. Melinda supports her career change goal with skills she's developed through school and a part-time job for a local builder. Her solid work history shows she's a responsible and contributing employee.

Lisa has had a successful career with a local bank, but she's decided, through her experience in mortgage loans, that she'd like to try a career in real estate. She has earned her real estate license and communicates her skills and related achievements in a functional resume. Note that Lisa lists additional training relevant to her new career. Although her college degree *isn't* career-related, it is a formal education, so she includes it.

Same company for several years, different jobs   76-77

Employees who have had several jobs with one company can state loudly and clearly that they are loyal, promotable employees, able to assume increased responsibilities. Both William and Meghan highlight their staying power by showing progression from entry-level to supervisory positions. They both quantify their achievements and detail how they contributed to the success of their organizations.

Combining two careers   78

Susan is fortunate to be talented in two areas—as a dental assistant and in sales management. Instead of working as a dental assistant full-time and trying to squeeze in part-time hours in sales, she's decided to combine two skills into one career as a dental sales representative. She successfully summarizes her dental skills and sales achievements and communicates how they would complement each other in her chosen profession. Note her quantified sales accomplishments.

Entry-level, ready to move up   79

Teresa's resume clearly and concisely states she has the experience, qualifications and skills necessary to assume a position with more responsibility. She has a solid background in all aspects of human resources and successfully presents her results-oriented achievements. Teresa wants prospective employers to understand she's looking for a management position, so she states that in her objective. She then supports her objective with solid human resources experience and by citing management skills such as budget planning, forecasting and program administration.

Seeking management position   80-81

In nine years, Monica has advanced from a temporary secretarial employee to a senior administrative assistant, and she isn't finished. To show she's qualified for a management position, she cites experience in budget planning, department goal-setting and program administration and development. Her track record proves that she can assume increased responsibility while posting excellent, quantifiable results. Although she doesn't have a college degree, she lists undergraduate studies in related fields and includes career-related memberships.

Small business owner seeking management position   82-83

Steven is self-employed and successfully highlights his managerial and organizational skills, business accomplishments, sales talents and supervisory and budgetary experience, all valuable qualifications for a management position. Notice that he uses an objective to clarify his career goal and quantifies results where possible. Steven also supports his international capabilities by citing specific work projects and noting he speaks

Spanish. He includes the positions he held before he started his own business to show potential employers he has corporate experience.

Job-hoppers, career-hoppers, relocaters, and those with little skills, fired or laid off

If your work history includes lots of jobs, lots of careers, lots of moving or limited skills, focus on the positive aspects of your career and neutralize the negative.

Individual who hasn't stayed at any job more than one year   84-85

Margaret hasn't been at any one job for more than one year, but that's because she's earned the reputation as a trouble-shooter who comes in, fixes the problem and moves on. She focuses on the positive by explaining she was recruited by each new employer, and that each position was a promotion. Margaret has solid, results-oriented achievements which reinforce her ability to solve problems. While she's not actively seeking another position, she keeps a current resume to share with recruiters.

Career-hopper   86-87

Steven has enjoyed a varied career in management, sales and politics, and has decided politics it is. After earning a master's degree in a related field and completing a legislative internship, he's ready to enter the arena. He lists his *new* career-related information first, including a clear objective, a skills profile and his education. His work history, though not related to his new career, is solid, results-oriented and shows he's a contributor. Note that Steven also has become involved in activities affiliated with his new field.

Young adult with some false starts   88

Paul has an erratic career history, but he's finally found his niche in warehouse operations. He's not currently looking for a new position, but he would like to move into management if something comes up. Although Paul is a job-hopper, he knows he may only raise suspicions by omitting employment dates, so he leaves them in. His accomplishments in warehouse operations help to overshadow his erratic work history.

Individual who's relocated a lot   89

Mark has relocated a lot, but since each move has been a promotion within the same company, his relocating isn't a negative. Mark mentions his general responsibilities and then covers each move independently, noting the outstanding accomplishments that led to his next promotion. His resume is an excellent example of results-oriented accomplishments.

Little training or skills   90

Anna may not have many skills or much training, but she's good at what she does, and she's earned awards for her work. Her strong employment history fits well into a chronological resume. (Those without a strong work history might opt for a functional resume.) Anna emphasizes her ability to enhance office operations and get the job done right and on time. Because she has no additional training, Anna includes her high school education.

Fired or laid off   91

Glenn was laid off or fired from a series of jobs before he hit his stride as a courier, and he'd like to stay in that area. He feels strongly about his capabilities and is prepared to answer questions about his somewhat erratic work history, so he uses a chronological resume. He avoids raising suspicions by including all dates.

Woman reentering job   92-93
market after raising children

Phyllis has some paid work experience, but she took time out to raise her children until they were all in school. Now she's ready to go back to teaching. Phyllis doesn't limit her resume to the teaching assignment she held 10 years ago. If she had, she would have left out valuable (and career-related) volunteer and instructional experience she took on as a result of her (and her children's) activities. She presents the picture of a well-rounded individual with mature professional experience, able to manage several responsibilities simultaneously.

Woman with erratic job history   94
due to husband's relocating

Gretchen's husband works for a major chemical company and has accepted promotions that have moved the family around the Midwest. However, because she is an excellent employee, Gretchen has found a position in each new city. She chose a functional resume to emphasize her skills and accomplishments and de-emphasize the number of employers she's had over the last 15 years. Notice how she ties in numbers to quantify her results.

Woman transferring volunteer   95
experience into work skills

Anne has never held a paid job, but look at the resume she's developed based on her volunteer experience with the library, church, school and community service organizations. She uses a functional resume to profile her excellent management and leadership skills and support her career goal. Note her results-oriented listings.

Woman entering traditionally   96
male field

Michelle is a mechanical engineer trying to advance in the automotive industry. She's been in the same position for five years now, and she's ready to move into project management. She chose a functional resume to emphasize her skills and downplay the fact she's really had only one job. Her skills headings are different than typical headings because of her chosen field, but they work well and support her career goal.

Older adults

Although it shouldn't be, age discrimination is a major concern for older working adults. If you fall into this category, experiment with a couple of options that can help you downplay your age but not your valuable contributions or mature experience.

Just remember omitting dates entirely *isn't* one of your options—that approach will only raise suspicions and perhaps make you appear older than you are.

Older woman with no paid job experience   97

Nancy is a recent widow in need of a steady income. While she has a solid and varied volunteer background, her strongest selling point is her catering experience. She put together a functional resume highlighting her excellent management and financial skills, essential qualifications in the food service business. She detracts from her age by including her number of years with each organization (instead of actual dates) and by omitting her graduation date.

Older adult coming out of retirement   98-99

Marcia successfully uses a functional resume to present her extensive professional background and downplay her age. By organizing her skills in career-related groupings, she proves she has the experience and qualifications necessary to support her career goal. Notice that she includes employment dates, but not until the end of the resume, after she's hooked the prospective employer and can capitalize on the value of her maturity.

Older adult changing careers   100-101

Mason is secure with his age and feels it's actually a benefit in his new career as an insurance agent. As an older adult, he understands what both young and old need in health and life insurance. Therefore, he includes all appropriate dates. He does, however, omit his first 20 years of employment—the work he did isn't relevant to his new career and is quite outdated. Instead, he includes positions that reflect his management and insurance-related experience.

Older male with management experience recently laid off   102

Anthony decided to address the age issue by omitting his first few jobs out of college. Work he performed during those years is obsolete in today's engineering world, anyway. He also omits his college graduation date—it was so long ago and definitely dates him. What remains is a solid resume with results-oriented information relevant to today's marketplace.

Individual who hasn't worked for a while   103

To avoid highlighting the fact that she hasn't worked for several years, Deborah chose a functional resume. Her experience is grouped by skills and emphasizes her strong organizational and administrative talents. She mentions results-oriented achievements where possible and includes her volunteer work. Deborah saves her experience listing for last, as her goal is to profile *what* she's achieved, not *where* and *when* she achieved it.

Military

Military duty provides excellent experience that translates well to the civilian job market...when accomplishments are phrased in nonmilitary terms. If you've served in the military, be careful to state your achievements in laymen's terms.

Military entering civilian market in different field   104-105

Sandra's military background has provided her with experience in a variety of areas, but she's chosen to pursue a career in teaching. Therefore, while she could have listed a number of accomplishments under each duty, she zeros in on instructional and training achievements. Sandra supports her career goal with substitute teaching assignments and other career-related activities.

Military entering civilian market   106-107

Edward has excellent aeronautical and supervisory experience, which he wants to apply in the civilian work force. His profile clearly states management and computer skills that will transfer well into the civilian business world. Notice how his noteworthy achievements are quantified and explained in laymen's terms.

High tech   108-111

With most resumes, it's important to use simple language, but high-tech jobs present a problem. When possible, translate high-tech information into laymen's terms. If you're in a high-tech field, chances are prospective employers understand the language. Also, many nontechnical human resources people are looking for buzzwords passed on by the direct manager. Sometimes, the work is so specialized that technical information can't be broken down and briefly explained.

For example, Linda's in a highly specialized area where she develops computer software involving the English language. To fully explain her accomplishments in laymen's terms would take five pages. In addition, most prospective employers she'd be contacting have experience in this area. Therefore, her resume contains highly technical language. Linda supports her qualifications with a list of publications, awards and patent information.

Marissa, on the other hand, is in a more generalized area and can somewhat "gear down" technical language. While she has a strong work history, she puts her education first to emphasize her MBA.

Notice her well-stated and quantified results. She includes a few outside activities to show she's more than just a "computer nerd."

Occupational resumes

The following occupational resumes are good examples for many of the same reasons: They are concise and clear. They address the employer's needs. They present quantifiable results. And they profile accomplishments. Each is briefly highlighted in its appropriate section.

Business and Professional

In general, a business or professional person should briefly summarize his or her level of responsibility and then highlight specific achievements.

Accounting   114-117

Gwen and Monica are both accountants, but Gwen emphasizes her cost accounting and auditing experience while Monica stresses her tax accounting and benefits planning achievements. Gwen also lists her computer skills immediately after her skills summary to draw attention to her knowledge of accounting software. Monica indicates her strong involvement in relevant professional affiliations, and both include supportive volunteer work.

Communications/PR   118-126

While resumes should always be clear and concise, communicators and public relations specialists are especially obligated to prepare well-written, well-organized resumes to reflect their communication skills.

Thomas covers his well-rounded background in most aspects of corporate communications and highlights major accomplishments at each job. He cites professional awards to support his claim as an award-winning writer. Tim first lists his experience with computer programs and systems necessary for success in his field. He then profiles his skills and talents with results-oriented achievements.

Douglas has a solid background in public information and emphasizes development and implementation of unique programs. He also outlines his editorial experience and includes continued education to complement his state agency experience.

Susana emphasizes her recent advanced degree by putting her education before her experience.

She supports a results-oriented resume with contributions to professional organizations. Lisa's resume reflects her ability to tailor information to specific groups and lead related workshops.

Paralegal 127

As a paralegal, Sandra's skills and certifications are most important, so she lists them first. You will also notice her results-oriented achievements and related affiliations, which support her capabilities.

Management 128-142

Managers need to emphasize their leadership qualities and ability to supervise people, budgets, production, programs, quality, operations and/or services. For example, Marianne's resume highlights her abilities in operations and service, while Wendy's profiles her experience with budgets and people, both essential skills in their chosen fields.

Gary communicates extensive experience in personnel and product management and emphasizes his ability to assume positions with increasing responsibility. He includes his college credit hours, even though he earned them some time ago, to show he does have some additional education.

Yee Su covers her achievements in innovative program development and management. She also cites experience in managing personnel and functions in field offices.

Timothy profiles his strengths in facility, personnel and production management and uses action words to communicate his leadership abilities. Susan uses results-oriented accomplishments to stress her office management skills and also features leadership abilities through policy development.

Miguel has been a manager only a few years, but he indicates how his extensive production background prepared and provided him with necessary skills and knowledge. Note his use of numbers to quantify results. Although he has no formal degree, he includes related studies to complement his achievements.

Cynthia highlights her leadership skills and how she applies them in managing employees to exceed production and financial goals. Edward emphasizes his accomplishments in manufacturing and quality control and profiles his ability to assume increased responsibility by making significant contributions.

Rosa conveys her ability to manage programs and client relations. Randall, a restaurant manager, mentions significant achievements in employee and service management and quantifies results with numbers. Note he also includes a management training program in his educational listing.

Administrative 143-144

Elaine and Carol detail how they lend administrative support. Elaine's experience is in middle-management office support, while

Carol typically assists in executive management projects. Elaine has solid work experience, but she includes her previous volunteer work and vocational schooling to support her skills.

Human Resources   145

Justin began his career in the military and successfully translates that experience into the civilian job market. He has continued to achieve quantified results and highlights his innovative contributions. Note that he also includes a career-related military honor.

Sales   146-150

Sales professionals will want to include numbers and percentages to quantify sales results, such as Theresa does. She also highlights computer skills and technical knowledge relevant to her sales area and includes a few activities to show she has outside interests.

Michael profiles his ability to develop services and programs to benefit customers and his employer. He includes supervisory and production experience to show additional management skills and lists a few activities to show he's a well-rounded individual.

Tammy's resume reveals her ability to accept increased responsibility and make valuable contributions. She includes her high school education because she has no formal education.

Analyst/Auditor   151-152

Margaret's experience is in long-range business planning, which she highlights and supports with quantifiable results. Although she has an advanced degree, she feels her work experience is solid and places it first.

Christina's resume shows how she advanced in her field in a relatively short period of time. She includes results-oriented achievements that brought her to her current position.

Other   153-156

Kenneth, a business owner, has compiled a resume to present to prospective investors. His accomplishments reflect his ability to determine and develop successful business expansions. Kenneth also includes professional activities to show additional involvement in his business area.

Brian has a somewhat unusual career but describes his responsibilities and highlights his achievements in laymen's terms. He uses numbers to quantify his results and profiles his contributions to successful business expansion.

Sara has solid experience, but she lists her computer languages and platforms first to alert prospective employers to her extensive knowledge. She then uses the employment section to emphasize specific accomplishments.

Education

158-163

Teachers may want to include an objective to identify the specific areas in which they wish to teach. Beginning teachers also should include their student teaching experiences. All teachers should list licensing information.

Abigail currently is teaching third grade, but she is licensed for kindergarten through third grade. To keep her options open, she includes all levels in her objective. Louise chose not to include an objective because her skills profile clearly indicates her specialty.

Notice how both of the teachers summarize their general teaching skills in their skills profiles and emphasize their achievements in their employment sections. Abigail is quite involved outside of the classroom, and she includes her many educational and instructional activities to convey her interests and her ability to handle several responsibilities.

As a school superintendent, Kevin has a solid background in implementing innovative school programs, and he briefly yet clearly highlights his numerous achievements. His professional activities relate his experience with a variety of educational organizations, and his community service shows that he is a well-rounded individual. He lists his many presentations on educational reform on a separate sheet.

Engineering

164-169

As with high-tech positions, many engineering fields have their own languages. Prospective employers will probably be familiar with those engineering terms, and human resources managers may be looking for certain buzz words, but don't take your chances. Translate engineering terms and accomplishments into laymen's terms.

Notice how all three resumes include some technical language but are still easily understood. Elisabeth and Gary use numbers to quantify their results. Jeanette has an extensive educational background and highlights her theses and publications to further emphasize her areas of specialty and knowledge.

Government, nonprofit, environmental, social service

Government   170-173

Government employees need to indicate their ability to work within the system but may want to consider emphasizing how those and other skills could apply to the civilian job market.

For example, Dennis works as an agricultural lender for a government agency, but he's interested in a job as a bank loan officer. In his summary, he states his experience in public administration and with government contracts, but his achievements emphasize his ability to develop and manage secure loan packages.

Amanda states her pharmacological experience with a government agency but also profiles her experience and accomplishments as a manager. Both people show how their skills would transfer into the civilian job market.

Nonprofit, environmental, social service   174-181

In general, nonprofit, environmental and social services professionals all work to benefit their communities and should be sure to profile those accomplishments.

Janet highlights her experience in establishing successful outreach programs for a needy community, including her ability to work with government agencies. Theresa built her nonprofit agency from scratch and uses figures to quantify her achievements.

As a legislative assistant, John is constantly working with the community and highlights his ability to determine and address local concerns and issues. He also indicates his experience in event planning and fund raising, both relevant skills in his field.

Anna and Jeanne highlight their talents in creating educational programs. Jeanne stresses her management skills. Anna includes her interest in Native American culture and her ability to speak Spanish, both of which she feels enhance her value in her field.

Although Nancy is an experienced social worker, she enjoys event planning and is a successful fund raiser. This information emphasizes her capabilities.

Health care, mental health

182-191

Health care and mental health workers should be sure to include their licensing and/or certification and any related training. Nurses also should include their intern/externships.

For example, Rebecca, Rhonda and Susan all have specific licenses or certifications that allow them to practice in their fields. Although Michael hasn't completed a formal degree, he includes related vocational training that many employers require for his position.

Note that Rebecca includes career-related volunteer experience and community memberships to complement her paid experience. Claire's resume emphasizes an all-around background in a variety of health care areas, showing her ability to "wear all hats," from public relations to contract negotiation.

While Omkar has solid, results-oriented experience, he also highlights his advanced degree, certification and involvement in professional organizations to support his work history.

Rhonda profiles her ability to develop specific, patient-related programs and provide award-winning care. Notice she also includes her student extern experience.

Susan summarizes specific skills and then lists her employment chronologically. She points out she did well in trade school while finishing high school and was honored as a top dental assistant.

Michael stresses his computer software skills, essential for his position. He also highlights managerial skills, including cutting expenses and establishing successful office management policies.

Skilled trades and others

Skilled trades   192-194

A skilled tradesperson's biggest selling point is his or her specialized skill. Be sure to mention any trade school degrees, appropriate licensing and related apprenticeships.

Scott, Patrick and Ronald first summarize their specific skills and then note specific acomplishments in their employment sections. Notice additional certification, licensing and training information.

Patrick and Ronald both have good examples of career-related interests. Ronald's employment background is varied, but he highlights current achievements and pulls out construction-related accomplishments to support his career goal.

Others   195-208

Nathan's career, both military and civilian, has centered around scheduling, organizing and coordinating goods and people. He ties that together in his skills summary and then highlights specific achievements under each position.

Kent's resume stresses his ability to develop and implement innovative public safety programs, but it also highlights management and organizational skills that would transfer well into the corporate job market. His activities and awards reveal his commitment to his community.

Natalie, Elizabeth, Victoria and Laura emphasize their abilities to develop age- and skill-appropriate children's programs. Natalie shows event planning and promotional abilities, while Elizabeth profiles management skills and related experience to support her career goal.

Victoria highlights her ability to place students with dance troupes and coordinate fund raising and special promotions. She includes performance and education to add to her accomplishments.

Laura's resume reveals that she's gaining career-related experience and initiating new programs while pursuing an associate's degree. She includes her GPA to show she can successfully juggle several responsibilities simultaneously.

Christopher's resume clearly states results-oriented accomplishments and shows his community involvement. He includes his GPA and work at his school's radio station in his list of achievements.

Leslie is an experienced designer who owns her own business. Most clients come to her by word of mouth, but she's created a resume to show to potential clients. She highlights specialized skills in restaurant planning and design, but includes residential achievements to show her well-rounded background.

Situational resumes

CHRISTOPHER MORROW

55 Center Drive • Coatsville, FL • 32310 • (305) 555-9745

SKILLS/ABILITIES

Organizational/Management
- Handled stocking and assisted in managing flow of stock in grocery store
- Prepared weekly inventory reports and submitted to supervisor
- Recommended new stocking system, which reduced stocking time by four hours a week
- Served as treasurer of high school RC airplane club for two years
- Coordinated candy sale fund raiser for RC airplane club, which resulted in $350 in profit
- Helped plan monthly "flyings" and quarterly meetings

Customer Relations
- Assisted grocery shoppers in finding products
- Provided carry-out service
- Created new customer comment program, which included a personal letter from the appropriate department head and increased customer satisfaction by 75%
- Served 78 customers on neighborhood newspaper route and handled billing and collections
- Initiated revised billing program for paper route, which increased on-time payments by 30%

Communication
- Wrote articles about RC airplane club for high school newspaper

WORK HISTORY

Stock clerk, Superthrift, Maddington, FL (Summers and after school, June 1992-current)
Newspaper carrier, *Daily Times*, Coatsville, FL (June 1990-June 1992)

EDUCATION

Graduate, Washington High School, Coatsville, FL (June 1994)

JUDY WATKINS
501 Terrace Lane
Huntsville, TX 77341
(409) 555-6623

Career goal   A secretarial or administrative assistant position.

Summary of skills

Organizational
- Worked with local business to update company's secretarial manual (fulfilled class requirement); helped design new memo format, which simplified formatting and gained company-wide acceptance.
- Created responsibilities manual for volunteers at county hospital, which reduced over-lapping duties and increased efficiency.
- Assisted in managing volunteers for outpatient information desk at hospital.

Secretarial
- Experienced in document formatting, proofreading and administrative assistant duties.
- Skilled in MicroSoft Works and Lotus 1-2-3 on IBM compatible system.
- Ability to type 70 words per minute with no errors.

Communication
- Delivered a speech to local civic clubs and philanthropic organizations on the importance of hospital volunteers, which brought in seven new volunteers.
- Wrote articles for local newspaper on vocational team's achievements at district and state contests.

Education

Graduation expected
June 1995
Huntsville High School, Huntsville, TX (Current GPA is 3.7/4.0)

Related course work
Bookkeeping I & II, Typing, Advanced Typing, Computer Operations, Word Processing I & II, Business Writing, Vocational Business Curriculum (2 years)

Awards
Outstanding High School Volunteer, Warren County Hospital (1995)
State Business Vocations Contest (1995)
- document formatting (1st)
- business knowledge (2nd)
- administrative assistant competition (2nd)

Memberships
Business Professionals of America (student member)
Texas Association of Hospital Volunteers
Jr. Rotarian

JANET MEYERS
1635 Elizabeth Drive
Worthington, OH 44203
(614) 555-4987

CAREER GOAL

A position as a sports reporter or city reporter for a daily metropolitan newspaper.

SUMMARY OF QUALIFICATIONS

- Experienced sports writer and editor
- Strong background in newspaper mechanics, layout and design
- Skilled in developing and implementing a variety of programs
- Well-developed organizational and leadership skills
- Familiarity with city government and how it operates

PROFESSIONAL EXPERIENCE

1993-1995

Staff, *The Exponent*, Purdue University, West Lafayette, IN
- Served as copy editor, assistant city desk editor and assistant sports editor for campus newspaper
- Assigned and covered city stories and sporting events
- Established "stringer" system among nonrevenue sports, which resulted in increased coverage of those sports in the newspaper
- Developed program matching city officials with newspaper reporters to enhance understanding of city government and its operations; resulted in more accurate coverage of council meetings and its decisions

1992-1995

Feature Writer, Purdue Sports Information Office, West Lafayette, IN
- Developed and implemented hometown feature program, which increased coverage of Purdue sports in athletes' local newspapers
- Wrote and placed nearly 50 articles throughout the United States
- Wrote three articles for the game-day football program

(continued)

**PROFESSIONAL
EXPERIENCE**
1989-1991

**Sports Reporter/High School Correspondent, *Daily Record*,
Worthington, OH**
- Covered community and high school sports for local newspaper
- Assisted with galley proofing and page layout
- Edited news releases for style and content

EDUCATION
May 1995

B.A. in Communications, Purdue University, West Lafayette, IN
- Graduated *With Distinction* (5.8/6.0)
- Earned minors in English and History
- Completed career-related courses in reporting, editing, ethics in
  journalism, communication law, newspaper layout and design,
  photography, radio and television, and magazine article writing

**CAMPUS
ACTIVITIES**

Purdue University All-American Marching Band
- Served as flag corps co-captain for three years
- Wrote at least three new routines for the 40-member flag corps
  each week and scheduled extra practices when necessary

Alpha Xi Delta National Sorority
- Completed terms as corresponding secretary, editor and choir
  director for college sorority
- Won national recognition for scrapbook layout, design and content
- Contributed quarterly feature and chapter highlights articles to
  national publication
- Organized "donate a window" program, encouraging alumni to
  purchase new windows for the chapter house

HONORS

- Alpha Lambda Delta Freshman Scholastic Honorary
- Sigma Delta Chi Journalism Honorary
- Skull and Crescent Leadership Honorary
- Worthington Area Panhellenic Scholarship Award (two years)

Recent college graduate
with job experience
Chronological

Michelle Lee • 21 College Ave., Apt. 6A • Lafayette, IN • 46099 • (317) 555-6126

Objective

Position as a veterinarian with a small animal practice, with emphasis in feline medicine and surgery.

Summary of Qualifications

Excellent training and experience in small animal surgery and treatment. Good background in office management and inventory control. Well-developed client relations skills.

Education

DVM, Purdue University School of Veterinary Medicine, West Lafayette, IN (5.7/6.0 GPA) (Expected May 1995)

Significant clerkship and course work: Clinical Pathology, Opthalmology/Small Animal Medicine, Small Animal Surgery, Client Relations, Non-Domestic Animal Medicine

Internship

Lakeside Animal Hospital, Sturgis, MI

(July-September 1994)

- Performed and assisted with small and large animal surgery.
- Managed office and medical supplies inventory.
- Assisted on farm calls and handled seven after-hours, large-animal emergencies.
- Recommended and implemented new computer software, which enhanced customer service and patient care by providing print-outs related to prescribed medication.

Work Experience

Animal Disease Diagnostic Lab, Purdue University

(September 1992-May 1994)

- Performed necropsies on a variety of species.

Sturgis Veterinary Clinic, Sturgis, MI

(Summers 1992, 1993)

- Completed small animal surgery, treatments and radiography.
- Performed clinical lab work and assisted on farm calls.
- Learned to work with clients, answer questions and address concerns.
- Supervised transition from manual to computerized record keeping, resulting in more accurate patient records and an enhanced annual check-up "reminder" program.

Lab Technician, Purdue University

(January-August 1991)

- Prepared and interpreted histopathology slides.
- Collected bovine blood samples.
- Ran reproductive hormonal assays.
- Implemented new report procedure, which provided clients with more detailed information.

TERRY LAWSON

65 N. Grant St. •. Salt Lake City, Utah • 84107 • (801) 555-1331

OBJECTIVE

An entry-level marketing or management position with a medium-sized business.

EDUCATION

Bachelor of Science, Business Administration, University of Utah, Salt Lake City
(Expected June 1995)
Major: Management
Minor: Marketing
Related course work: personnel management, business management, business ethics, business
law, macro economics, statistics, marketing and sales

SKILLS/ABILITIES

Management

- Developed and implemented new fund-raising program for social fraternity, which brought in more than $1,500 for local charity
- Worked with local and national alumni chapters to coordinate chapter house expansion, including negotiating a construction contract and schedule
- Organized and communicated to chapter alumni about a house expansion fund-raising program, which to date has brought in enough to cover 50% of expansion costs
- Managed chapter house finances for two years, including collecting dues and paying bills
- Carried a full courseload while serving as chapter officer and working on campus newspaper advertising staff

Sales

- Led campus newspaper advertising staff three consecutive years for most advertising dollars generated
- Organized and implemented advertising promotion, which increased number of advertisers by 45%

Communication

- Presented monthly financial reports to chapter members and quarterly reports to national headquarters
- Corresponded with chapter alumni on progress of house expansion and fund raiser

Leadership

- Served as fraternity president, business manager and social chairman
- Named to Skull and Crescent National Leadership Honorary

EXPERIENCE

Advertising Staff, *Utah Extra*, University of Utah, Salt Lake (September 1991- current)
Business Manager, Sigma Chi, University of Utah, Salt Lake (September 1993 - May 1994)

Individual who's earned college
degree in mid-career
Chronological

BRIDGETTE T. LARSON

52 N. State St.
Stilesville, NH 03472
(603) 555-9232

CAREER OBJECTIVE

To secure a full-time teaching position at the kindergarten to third-grade level.

EDUCATION/LICENSING

Bachelor of Science Degree, Early Childhood Education, University of New Hampshire, Bedford (May 1994)
New Hampshire State License in Elementary Education (June 1994)

PROFILE

- Extensive background in early childhood care and education
- Skilled in developing and implementing lesson plans for all areas of a developmentally appropriate curriculum
- Able to create and initiate hands-on learning experiences
- Experienced in designing and implementing integrated learning centers
- Knowledge and confidence to advise and counsel parents on their child's specific cognitive or emotional problems
- Skilled day care and business manager

STUDENT TEACHING

Student Teacher, Bedford Elementary School, Bedford, NH (March-May 1993)
- Developed and implemented lesson plans for all areas of the third-grade curriculum
- Established activity/reading center, which provided materials for and challenged students who finished class assignments ahead of others
- Created, graded and recorded academic progress tests
- Assisted classroom teacher in organizing three field trips

Student Teacher, Bedford Elementary School, Bedford, NH (February-March 1993)
- Created and implemented lesson plans for 39 kindergarten students during the six-week teaching assignment
- Designed and implemented integrated learning centers on dinosaurs and ocean life
- Incorporated sand and water table play into the classroom, which encouraged hands-on learning

(continued)

CURRENT INSTRUCTIONAL EXPERIENCE

Substitute Teacher, Stilesville Community School Corporation, Stilesville, NH (September 1994-current)
- Guide students through lesson plans set by teacher
- Help students prepare and organize for classroom lessons/activities and hold them accountable for their work
- Assist students in reviewing for exams and completing homework assignments
- Maintain disciplined academic atmosphere
- Created and gained acceptance for Substitute Teacher's Handbook, which details how to handle substitute assignments, answers common questions and addresses potential classroom problems

Volunteer Tutor, Bedford Public Library, Bedford, NH (June 1993-current)
- Tutor kindergarten through third-grade students in reading
- Work with up to four children each month
- Assisted in mainstreaming three remedial reading students into regular reading classrooms

Owner/Administrator/Teacher, Wee Care Day Care/Nursery School, Stilesville, NH
(January 1983-current)
- Opened to meet the need for quality, developmentally appropriate day care for two- to 10-year-old children in the community
- Expanded in October 1986 to include infants and toddlers
- Began nursery school program in September 1988 to address needs for stay-at-home parents
- Provide annual day care for up to 75 children, with more than 125 students enrolled in various programs
- Offer developmentally appropriate curriculum, including field trips, guest speakers and hands-on learning experiences for all ages
- Participate in community events, such as the Fourth of July parade, home basketball games and holiday programs
- Manage staff of 12

ADDITIONAL ACTIVITIES

Church School Teacher, St. Joseph Church, Stilesville, NH
Leader, Girl Scout Child Care Project, Stiles County, NH

Individual who's earned advanced
degree in mid-career
Chronological

Lori T. Childers
455 Bennington Circle
Atlanta, GA 30332
(404) 555-2003

PROFILE

Solid background in financial analysis and marketing, with strong emphasis in telecommunications account management. Consistently exceed sales goals and customer service expectations. Experienced in handling international accounts and in presenting results of consortium operations. Skilled in developing and implementing standardized policies and procedures.

EDUCATION

M.B.A. Marketing, Georgia Tech University, Atlanta, May 1995
B.S. Accounting, University of Nebraska, Lincoln, May 1984

CAREER HISTORY

Sept 1993-current

Gulf Telephone, Large Business Marketing, Atlanta, GA
Corporate Account Manager
- Exceed sales goals each year, including 150% of goal for 1995
- Manage five-member account team to serve large business customers
- Consistently earn highest rating in customer service quality surveys
- Coordinated and responded to complex customer telecommunications requests, resulting in increased sales and customer satisfaction
- Sold and worked with a variety of Gulf Telephone products and network and integration services, including SMDS, ISDN, video conferencing, routers, CPEs and multiplexers
- Closed the largest network integration sale ever, scored a competitive winback from AT&T, and sold an ISDN data network to a major customer with 150 sites

March 1989-Sept 1993

Gulf Telephone International, Inc., Atlanta, GA
Financial Manager
- Handled financial analysis and reporting of corporate finances, including activities in the Caribbean
- Managed finances for domestic and international projects
- Developed and implemented policies and procedures over financial transactions, resulting in standardized reports
- Coordinated relationships with other Gulf Telephone finance departments, which helped standardize procedures across all operating groups

May 1984-March 1989

Specter, Williams and Ritz, Atlanta, GA
Senior Accountant
- Managed audit team that performed commercial financial statement audits
- Planned, budgeted and supervised engagements in excess of 800 hours
- Developed and implemented client service program, which expanded small-to-medium client base 35%
- Served government contractors and other commercial customers

Emilio Sanchez
32 Westview Blvd., Apt. 5
Circleville, CT 00345
(203) 555-2003

Profile

Skilled research engineer with doctorate in materials engineering. Strong background in manufacturing process development and in product improvement programs. Experienced in managing projects from conception to completion.

Education

Doctorate of Philosophy, University of Connecticut (1994)
Dissertation topic: Alloy modifications to Deotel 61 to reduce additions of strategic elements while retaining the original material properties

Master of Science, Massachusetts Institute of Technology (1992)
Theses topic: Optimizing the structure and properties of advanced cast irons to improve thermal fatigue resistance

Bachelor of Science, New York University (1990)

Publications

Doctoral Dissertation
Sanchez, *Metallurgy and Properties Research*, Pressman Publishers, 1995.

Master's Thesis
Sanchez, *National Foundryman's Journal*, Wolcott & Associates, 1993.

Invited Paper/Presentation
"Improved Product Performance through Application of High-Strength Steels, Advanced Aluminum Alloys, Metal and Polymer Composites and Ceramics," 1995 International Tool Manufacturing Show, New York City, NY

Experience

June 1992-current

Research Engineer, Warren Industries, Stamford, CT
Manage projects for several externally sponsored and company-funded manufacturing development programs.
- Handle the entire spectrum of the traditional material removal processes, nonconventional techniques, tool design, process design and expert systems
- Manage projects from conception through development planning, budgeting and scheduling; supervise technicians; present program highlights at executive conferences and trade shows
- Revised research process to better coordinate with product marketing, resulting in more successful marketing programs and increased sales

Sept 1992-May 1994

Professor's Assistant, Massachusetts Institute of Technology
Assisted and instructed undergraduate students in classroom and laboratory settings.
- Created all lecture and semester and final exam materials
- Helped revise curriculum and graduation requirements for materials engineering students to better prepare them for the job market

JAMES L. BENDER
701 Morningside Dr.
Woodland, MI 49003
(313) 555-2339

SKILLS PROFILE

- Manager with extensive background in quality control.
- Skilled in counseling customers on quality issues, establishing quality standards and solving quality-related problems.
- Experienced in meeting audit and survey requirements of current and prospective customers and in auditing suppliers to ensure conformance to customer specifications.
- Skilled in writing and maintaining quality manuals and in writing work instructions, quality procedures, in-process and final inspection forms.

WORK EXPERIENCE

May 1991-current

Quality Manager, Ridgeway Engineering, Detroit, MI
Manage internal quality of manufacturing records, certifications and requirements of individual customers. Supervise three inspectors.

- Handle internal and supplier audits, gauge calibration and implementation of SPC.
- Raised quality rating with major customer from 60% to 100% in two years and have had no rejections in three years.
- Earned Certified Supplier status with major customer and achieved no-inspection status for goods shipped from production plant to customer plant.
- Recommended and implemented new process, which increased production by 25% without jeopardizing quality.

Oct 1986-Oct 1991

Inspection Supervisor, Tube Forming, Corp., Woodland, MI

- Inspected in-process, welding, flouropenetrant and final assembly.
- Handled fabrication, layout of aircraft engine tubing and components for G.E., Allison and Pratt & Whitney.
- Implemented new inspection process, which identified and led to correction of potential defects.

(continued)

WORK EXPERIENCE

Jan 1986-June 1988

Production Supervisor, Transmission Suppliers, Inc., Woodland, MI
Supervised manufacturing and grinding of friction wafers for bonding to clutch and transmission parts. Met tolerances of ±001.
- Used standard micrometers along with electronic mikes capable of averaging and SPC.
- Recommended new process, resulting in fewer casting cracks, higher product quality and $2 million in new business.
- Established new production procedure, which increased units produced by 40%.
- Wrote new quality manual, which established product specifications and standards necessary to meet customer requirements.

June 1984-Jan 1986

Purchasing Agent/Shop Supervisor, Ridenour Systems, Detroit, MI
Ordered and received materials. Controlled inventory. Supervised shop crew of six.
- Recommended new purchasing system, which eliminated delays, reduced paperwork and enhanced inventory control.
- Established standardized shop procedures, which resulted in more efficient operations and reduced training time.

June 1979-June 1982

Machinist, National Filters, Detroit, MI
Set up and operated engine and turret lathes, radial drills, milling machines and bullards. Inspected with tolerances of $\pm.001$. Served as group leader.
- Initiated new shop safety procedure, which reduced on-the-job injuries by 45%.

EDUCATION

Technical Vocational College, Woodland, MI (1987)
- Mechanical Drafting
- Machine Shop Supervision

National Filters, Detroit, MI (1980)
- Machine Shop
- Drafting

Michigan State University (1978-1979)
- General Studies

Martin S. Feeney
530 Winding Way
Gray Lake, MN 55735
(612) 555-2003

Objective

A full-time position as a music teacher at the elementary level.

Summary of Skills
- Teaching license with endorsement in musical instruction.
- Experience in tutoring elementary-aged children.
- Solid background as accompanist and assistant choral director.
- Skilled in designing hands-on learning centers.
- Ability to maintain discipline in the classroom while allowing children the freedom to discover the world of music.

Instructional Experience

Private Piano Instructor, Gray Lake, MN (1991 - current)
- Instruct 10 students in piano and the basics of learning and performing music.
- Host annual recital for students.
- Wrote and published instructional manual for beginning piano students.

Student Teacher, Gray Lake Elementary School and Warren Memorial Elementary School, Gray Lake School District, Gray Lake, MN (January - March 1995)
- Created daily lesson plans incorporating a variety of choral and instrumental music experiences for kindergarten through fifth-grade students in two schools.
- Worked with lead teacher to design a modified program for physically challenged students.
- Established program where students visit local nursing home to meet residents and teach them songs, providing a special activity for the residents and a learning/musical experience for the children.
- Created learning centers combining experiences in music and math.

Tutor, Minnesota State University, East Ridge, MN (1987 - 1989)
- Provided elementary-aged children with one-on-one education in math and reading.
- Worked with teachers to streamline two children from remedial to regular reading classes.

(continued)

Musical Experience

Accompanist, Children's Choir, St. Luke's Methodist Church, Gray Lake, MN (1992 - current)
- Provide piano accompaniment for 20-member choir.
- Initiated instruction in rhythm instruments, which children now use to accompany their musical presentations.

Assistant Choral Director, Chancel Choir, St. Luke's Methodist Church, Gray Lake, MN (1993 - current)
- Assist in selecting appropriate music for weekly worship services.
- Assist in directing choir during worship services.
- Initiated and direct combined handbell choir/chancel choir musical selections.

Orchestra member, Lakeview Community Theatre, Lakeview, MN (1994 - 1995)
- Provide keyboard accompaniment for two summer presentations.

Other Employment History

Account Analyst, Brownbury Financial Services, Minot, MN (1993 - current)
- Analyze and adjust accounts, including applying deferments and forbearances.
- Manually figure borrower and government interest for approximately 65 accounts per day.
- Served on team that recommended computer system upgrade, which enhanced system operation and reduced "bugs" and system "hang-ups."

Customer Service Representative, First National Bank, Minot, MN (1991 - 1993)
- Discussed available products, investigated account inquiries and answered customer service questions for approximately 100 customers daily.
- Assisted in training new service representatives.
- Revised filing system to accommodate centralization of customer service operations and provide easy filing/access for all new incoming correspondence.

Teller, First National Bank, Lakeview, MN (1989 - 1991)
- Accepted deposits, cashed checks and balanced teller window.
- Helped balance and maintain branch's daily records.
- Trained all part-time tellers.
- Recommended new verification process, which reduced customer account adjustment activity.

Education/Licensing

B.S. in Education, Otterbein University, Hudson, MN (1995)
Endorsement in Musical Instruction

State of Minnesota Teachers License (1995)

B.S. in Liberal Arts, Minnesota State University, East Ridge, MN (1989)

Melinda Price

505 E. Main St.
Shelbyville, TN 37160
(916) 555-2994

CAREER OBJECTIVE

Home designer for a major residential builder/developer

SKILLS PROFILE

- Well-developed drafting and technical skills
- Experience coordinating and managing subcontractors
- Knowledge of–and experience in–rezoning and meeting code specifications
- Excellent problem-solving skills
- Solid business and management background

EDUCATION

Associate's Degree in Architectural Technology, Tennessee University School of Science and Technology (1995)

ASSOCIATIONS/AWARDS

American Association of Architectural Engineers (1995 - current)
Honorable Mention, Best New Home Designer, Tennessee Architectural Society (1995)

EMPLOYMENT HISTORY

Home Designer, Browning Residence, Inc., Shelbyville, TN (1995 - current, part-time)
- Perform drafting and technical work for residential and commercial projects
- Recommended and established new subcontracting procedure, which has reduced construction delays
- Handle all rezoning and code specifications in commercial projects

Branch Manager, First National Bank, Knoxville, TN (1990 - current)
- Supervised branch operations, new account personnel and the investment department
- Guided branch through successful conversion to new computer system, products and procedures, resulting in fewer teller errors, faster posting and more efficient operations

Senior Teller, First National Bank, Knoxville, TN (1988 - 1990)
- Assisted branch manager with all banking operations
- Completed all teller work, including ensuring other tellers complied with proper procedures and adhered to policy changes
- Established new computerized consumer loan process with main branch, which reduced paperwork and approval time

Teller, First National Bank, Knoxville, TN (1985 - 1988)
- Provided customer service and new accounts service
- Served as back-up to loan and investment departments

LISA MAYS
80 West 106th St.
Templeton, KY 42351
(502) 555-3945

CAREER OBJECTIVE   Agent with a regional real estate firm.

SUMMARY OF QUALIFICATIONS

Communication/Marketing Skills
- Designed customer information guide for first-time home buyers, which enhances bank's image as knowledgeable lender.
- Nearly 70% of customers who visit bank and take brochure return for mortgage loan, although bank not always offering lowest lending rates.
- Addressed market demand by developing automated withdrawal procedure for payments on bank-held mortgages.
- Handled retail sales for floral designer and introduced new gift line that increased sales 25%.

Leadership Skills
- Served on team that tripled mortgage turnover for bank.
- Recommended, adapted and entered loan processing functions into computer system, resulting in faster approval time.
- Recommended new computer software that improved posting time and decreased errors.

Financial Skills
- Thorough knowledge of mortgage loans, points and interest, and how they affect the buyer.
- Process mortgage loans, including FHA and VA loans.

EMPLOYMENT   **Mortgage Loan Processor**, First National Bank, Templeton, KY (April 1992-present)
Bookkeeper, First National Bank, Templeton, KY (Feb 1989-April 1992)
Floral Designer/Sales Clerk, Whitmer's Flowers and Gifts, Nora, KY
(June 1987-Feb 1989)

EDUCATION/LICENSING

1995	Real Estate License, State of Kentucky
1994, 1991	Division of Continuing Studies, Cutter University, Akron, KY
	Courses in real estate law (1994) and data processing (1991)
1993	National Banking Institute, Frankfort, KY
	Courses in FHA and VA loan processing
1987	A.S. Degree in Horticulture, Cutter University, Akron, KY

Individual with same company for
several years but in different jobs
Chronological

WILLIAM J. BENNETT
725 Otter Lane
Wausau, WI 54554
(715) 555-6006

SKILLS SUMMARY

Skilled executive with extensive background in—and thorough knowledge of—bank operations and mortgage, commercial and consumer lending. Experienced in developing and implementing competitive programs and services. Exceptional organizational, analytical and managerial skills.

EXPERIENCE
June 1979-current

First City Bank, Wausau, WI
Vice President, January 1991-current
* Supervise 60 employees and total bank operations for main office and three branches with a total of $50 million in assets.
* Developed and continue to implement new business development plan, which includes calling on customers and prospects while enhancing bank's image in the community.
* Established new IRA procedures and Discount Brokerage Service, which expanded customer service offerings and created new business.

Manager, March 1987-January 1991
* Performed branch employee evaluations, scheduled continued education and training and assisted with career and sales development.
* Managed all daily branch operations, including opening and closing of branch, implementing and maintaining policies and procedures, ensuring compliance with federal banking regulations, customer contact and conflict resolution, and overdraft authorization.
* Developed and implemented bank's enhanced automated teller machine system, which provided a new, high-tech, competitive service.

Loan Officer, October 1984-March 1987
* Developed, originated, documented and closed commercial, consumer and mortgage loans, concentrating in residential construction lending and commercial lending.
* Expanded business development to include deposits and loans, which increased loan business 25%.
* Developed and implemented indirect lending program, which filled a need as identified by customer feedback.

Assistant Branch Manager, June 1979-October 1984
* Handled most daily branch operations and trained all new employees.
* Supervised successful conversion from manual to computerized record-keeping, resulting in enhanced customer service and account reporting.
* Coordinated construction and on-schedule completion of new branch.

EDUCATION

B.S. in Business Management, University of Wisconsin, Beloit (1979)

Individual with same company for
several years but in different jobs
Chronological

Meghan S. Wilgus
505 W. Delaware
Hagerstown, MD 21741
(301) 555-1221

Profile

More than 10 years experience in production supervision, with special emphasis on scheduling. Skilled in personnel supervision, training and vendor relations. Adept at revising current processes to improve plant operations.

Work History
June 1985-current

Waverly Industries, Hagerstown, MD
Production Control Supervisor (February 1992-current)
Supervise and train up to eight production schedulers in machine shop, polishing and assembly departments. Create daily and weekly device schedules based on monthly master schedule output.
- Initiated duty to serve as material dispatcher and outside vendor contact, which provides link between operations and has resulted in improved vendor relations and long-term contracts from three major vendors.
- Designed new assembly process for product, which reduced assembly time 30% and increased production 50%, without jeopardizing quality.

Production Scheduler-Assembly (October 1989-February 1992)
Created daily device dispatch list and procured material from shop floor and warehouse for dispatch list.
- Worked with machine shop, polishing and plating departments to revise procedures, resulting in smooth material flow through manufacturing plant.

Master Production Scheduler (May 1987-October 1989)
Created and maintained master production schedule for all "push pad" devices on monthly basis, using backlog, forecasts and historical data.
- Devised daily update system for master schedule, which provided additional scheduling information by logging return of completed dispatch list from shop floor.
- Initiated evaluation of item master maintenance and system de-bugging, which resulted in error-free, standardized coding system.

Project Engineer (June 1985-May 1987)
Created and maintained product data management concerning all shop routings, time studies, tooling and other information.
- Brought several vendor operations in-house, resulting in annual savings of $200,000.

Education

B.S. in Industrial Management, University of Maryland, College Park, 1985

Activities

Secretary, Maryland Businesswomen's Association, Hagerstown Chapter
Board Member, Boys' and Girls' Club of Hagerstown

SUSAN J. SMOCK

24 Countryside Lane   (702) 555-9776
Jackson, NV 89934

OBJECTIVE   A position as a sales representative or account manager with a major dental products supplier.

SUMMARY OF SKILLS

- Extensive training and experience in expanded dental assistant duties
- Thorough knowledge of dental hygiene products and their use in proper oral hygiene and soft tissue management
- Experienced in encouraging and "selling" quality, preventive dentistry to patients
- Strong and successful background in retail sales, purchasing and management
- Skilled in organizing and presenting product seminars

DENTAL EXPERIENCE

Jan 1992-current   Expanded Duties Dental Assistant, Dr. Eric L. Hussong, DDS, Jackson, NV
Jan 1989-Jan 1992   Expanded Duties Dental Assistant, Dr. Brenda S. Walker, DDS, Silverton, NV

SALES EXPERIENCE

Jan 1989-current   Sales Clerk, Sarah's Boutique, Jackson, NV
- Handle floor sales and assist and advise customers in selecting purchases
- Design innovative window displays, which increase customer traffic in store
- Recommended and implemented introduction of new sportswear line, which increased sales 25%
- Created new sales promotion, which increased ready-to-wear sales 35%

June 1985-Dec 1988   Sales Manager, The Silver Box, Silverton, NV
- Completed sales and purchasing duties for women's clothing store
- Created and implemented new, upscale "look" for store, including new floor plan, display ideas and logo
- Introduced new shopping service using customer profile program, which allowed for gift purchases by telephone and increased sales 15%
- Consistently exceeded sales objectives by at least 30%
- Assumed additional responsibility and assisted in business expansion by managing all purchases for new store in nearby community

CERTIFICATION

1988   Expanded Duties Certification, Nevada University School of Dentistry, Carson City

Young adult with entry-level
experience wanting to move up
Chronological

Teresa Seguso • 501 Hampton Dr. • Lakeview, KY • 40990 • (502) 555-9223

Objective

A position as human resources manager of a company with 1,200-plus employees.

Summary of Qualifications

Excellent human resources background, including: applicant screening; employee orientation, evaluation and placement; safety and training; and benefits planning. Experienced in developing and implementing new safety, training and employee orientation programs.

Work Experience

Human Resources Assistant, Allied Associates, Lakeview, KY

(March 1994-current)

- Designed new employee orientation package and established and facilitated all new employee activities and sessions, which provides (for the first time) continuity in all company and benefit information presented verbally and in writing.
- Assist vice president in budget reconciliation and other forecasting/planning activities.
- Assisted in administering a revised employee evaluation program, which allows for improvement on identified problem areas before final evaluation.
- Prepare confidential material for grievance and other personnel-related meetings.
- Researched and currently implementing flex benefits program, which allows employees to design their own benefits packages, resulting in higher employee satisfaction.

Training and Safety Assistant, McMurtry and Co., Lexington, KY

(October 1992-March 1994)

- Worked with training manager to develop new, in-house computer software training courses, saving $3,500 annually in outside training costs.
- Assisted training manager in developing Secretarial Training Program, which has successfully standardized procedures and enhanced office work flow.
- Revised safety manual and initiated OSHA update bulletins, which reduced on-the-job injuries by 55% and reduced OSHA non-compliance warnings by 75%.
- Assisted in evaluating and scheduling all outside executive training programs.

Personnel Assistant, McMurtry and Co., Lexington, KY

(May 1990-October 1992)

- Administered temporary service personnel program, which involved 40% of the secretarial and hourly work force on site.
- Scheduled and screened full-time job applicants and coordinated applicant testing and pre-employment physicals.
- Established and administered service award program.
- Created job descriptions for hourly employees.

Education

B.S. in Business Administration, University of Kentucky, Lexington (1990)

MONICA GREEN
37 Bayberry Court
Gateway, GA 30372
(404) 555-4299

SKILLS PROFILE

- Well-rounded background in human resources, training, safety, operations and consumer affairs.
- Excellent experience developing and implementing a variety of corporate programs, including those that must comply with corporate, state and/or federal agency guidelines.
- Skilled in developing department budgets and creating department objectives.
- Experienced in writing and delivering presentations for executive meetings.

WORK HISTORY

July 1993-present

Sr. Administrative Assistant, Operations & Safety, Ralston Corp., Atlanta, GA

- Develop yearly budgetary forecasts for three departments and ensure forecasts meet corporate guidelines.
- Served on team that created short- and long-term department objectives in accordance with company goals.
- Administer safety program at local plant and work with safety coordinators at company's three other plants to address safety issues presented by employees.
- Updated and implemented safety training program for product manufacturing groups at all plants, which reduced on-the-job injuries by 75%.
- Maintain OSHA log, analyze incidents at local site and review proposed regulations for impact on local plant.

June 1988-July 1993

Consumer Affairs Specialist, Ralston Corp., Atlanta, GA

- Initiated new tracking system to follow up consumer letters sent to other departments for response; response time to consumer increased by 50%.
- Achieved top ranking among eight other team members for toll-free number performance (efficiency and effectiveness in handling consumer calls).
- Prepared quarterly reports, graphs and quality assurance grids for two products.
- Developed Degradability Response Letter and drafted microwave, degradability and recycling information for product packages.

(continued)

WORK HISTORY

March 1987-June 1988

Secretary/Personnel Assistant, Human Resources, Ralston Corp., Atlanta, GA
- Worked with training manager to develop and implement New Employee Orientation Program (NEOP).
- Wrote New Employee Reference Guide, which helped employees better understand the company, its operations and who to contact with questions.
- Assisted training manager in developing Secretarial Training Program, resulting in a more efficient, productive staff.
- Assisted vice president in budget reconciliation and other activities.

January 1986-March 1987

Human Resources Clerk, Goodman and Sons, Inc., Waverly, GA
- Scheduled full-time job applicants and coordinated applicant testing and pre-employment physicals.
- Created and implemented service award program, including determining and ordering awards for years of service and supplying information to company newsletter.
- Assisted in introducing flex benefits program and facilitated employee meetings, which helped gain employee acceptance.

June 1984-January 1986

Confidential Temporary, McClure Temporary Services, Atlanta, GA
- Worked primarily in personnel departments of larger companies, handling information related to full-time job applicants.
- Created, updated and verified clerical job descriptions with appropriate department heads.

EDUCATION

1993-current
Undergraduate studies in Business Administration, Beacom College, Atlanta, GA

1982-1984
Undergraduate studies in Personnel Management, Beacom College, Atlanta, GA

ACTIVITIES/MEMBERSHIPS

- Treasurer, Ralston Activities Committee
- Member, Society of Consumer Affairs Professionals
- Member, National Association of Personnel Women

STEVEN T. HAWKINS
602 Brandenway Court
Williams, CA 95510
(707) 555-8324

Objective: To apply small business and international experience to corporate management position.

Profile: Self-employed construction project manager with extensive supervisory and carpentry background. Successfully operated own businesses for 15 years, including completing and winning major bids, managing a labor force and finishing projects on schedule and on budget. Experienced at supervising and completing projects in other countries. Can converse in Spanish.

Work Experience:

March 1984 - present   **Owner/Manager, Hawkins Enterprises, Williams, CA**
Complete interior finish projects, including submitting bids, supervising operations, hiring and training labor, purchasing materials and handling payroll and customer relations.
- Trained local labor force, supervised product shipment and successfully managed projects in France, Hong Kong and Ecuador, completing all projects on time and on budget.
- Successfully bid for and completed various interior projects for financial institutions and small and large businesses in two-state area.
- Completed eight spec houses in the $800,000 range.
- Completed a variety of general construction projects involving residential remodeling and agricultural facilities.

August 1981 -
March 1984   **Owner/Manager, Movable Walls, Rosewood, CA**
Completed interior finish projects for national company dealing in movable wall partitions.
- Established installation capabilities for national dealer in three-state area, resulting in 40% sales increase for dealer and 46 new major business opportunities.
- Completed 32 projects for small and large businesses.
- Hired and trained own labor force.

August 1977 -
August 1981   **Interiors, Inc., Rosewood, CA**
Area Manager
Expanded market for movable wall partitions throughout northern California.
- Consulted with prospective clients and provided cost, benefits and installation schedule information, creating new markets and increasing sales 35%.
- Managed a six-person field staff and two-person office staff.
- Personally supervised 26 projects.

(continued)

Work Experience:

August 1977 -
August 1981

Installation Training Manager
Supervised training program for company installers and supervisors.
* Developed and implemented new training manual and training program, resulting in more efficient, produtive installers, higher customer satisfaction and fewer design errors.
* Served as member of product development team, which created 10 standard, easy-to-install office designs to meet small-office market demands.

January 1974 -
August 1977

Hickman Co., Greenville, CA
Carpenter Foreman
Managed construction projects in northern California and western Nevada.
* Successfully completed 25 major projects on time.
* Supervised union carpenters.
* Secured seven new construction projects for the company.

August 1974 -
September 1975

Skilled Carpenter (self-employed), Wooster, CA
* Completed general construction and specialty trim work.
* Recommended new trim technique, which reduced finishing time and material costs and increased durability.
* Remodeled own Victorian home to original design and appearance.

Education:

Associate's Degree in Supervision, University of Northern California (1977)
Associate's Degree in Business Management, State Community College (1982)

Memberships:

West Coast Carpenter's Association, area representative (1985-1988)

Individual who hasn't stayed at any
job for more than one year
Chronological

MARGARET K. COOPER
1815 W. Barner St.
Anchorage, AK 99506
(907) 555-6887

SKILLS SUMMARY

Supervisor with seven years accounting experience in medical billing, collections and patient payment plans. Solid background in computer software, computer operations and training. Consistently recruited to trouble-shoot and establish billing/collection policies and procedures.

PROFESSIONAL EXPERIENCE

March 1995-current

Patient Accounts Manager, Chugach Orthopedics, P.C., Anchorage, AK
Supervise three employees in billing office for four orthopedic surgeons. Arrange financial payment plans with patients and set up in-house collection policies.
- Recruited to reorganize billing office and establish new job responsibilities to improve work flow and create opportunities for cross-training and career development.
- Apprise front and back office staff on all current insurance policies and requirements.
- Renew physicians' credentials with contracted PPOs, HMOs and other networks.
- Established new collection and patient payment policies, which have reduced uncollected bills by 35%.

April 1994-March 1995

Account Analyst, Union Hospital Physician Billing Office, Anchorage, AK
Maintained two deposit reports. Managed money for 14 physicians, including all current over-the-counter collections.
- Assumed temporary position to assist in training 30 employees in registration and scheduling on new computer software system.
- Hired, trained and supervised temporary employees on old computer system.
- Supervised temporary employees for collection of old accounts receivable.

June 1993-April 1994

Business Office Manager, Anchorage General Hospital, Anchorage, AK
Supervised nine employees, including front office, billing, collections, payroll and admissions personnel.
- Hired to revise procedures for collecting patient and insurance portions of patient accounts; reduced turnaround from nine weeks to two.
- Handled all daily deposits, audited general ledger and prepared month-end reports.
- Conducted financial interviews with patients still in-house.

(continued)

**PROFESSIONAL
EXPERIENCE**

May 1992-June 1993   **Accounts Receivable Manager,** Bayside Medical Group, Fairbanks, AK
Supervised six employees in billing office for 14 physicians. Managed
office's computer operation, including training staff on accounting software.
* Recruited to establish and manage billing and collections for satellite
  Occupational Health office, posting 98% collection rate.
* Processed refunds and prepared all accounts receivable reports.

May 1991-May 1992   **Accounting Assistant,** Yukon Hospital, Fairbanks, AK
Handled data processing, including computer input of cash, charges,
adjustments, daily census and admissions.
* Assumed temporary position to supervise all data input for new software
  program.

June 1990-May 1991   **Accounts Payable Clerk,** Hobson Living Centers, Seattle, WA
Edited and batched invoices from 15 nursing homes.
* Conducted training seminars for 15 out-of-state nursing homes.

June 1989-June 1990   **Internal Audit Clerk,** Hobson Living Centers, Seattle, WA
Audited patients' personal funds and audited payables to general ledger.
Served as secretary to field analyst.
* Promoted after one year.

EDUCATION   Associate's Degree in Accounting, Lincoln Community College, WA (1988)

ACTIVITIES   Volunteer, English Estates Nursing Home and Adult Day Care, Anchorage
Math Tutor, Gannett Elementary School, Anchorage

STEVEN R. RHOADES
401 Brightwood Dr.
Glen Ellyn, IL 60312
(708) 555-3565

CAREER GOAL

To secure a position with a U.S. Senator's or U.S. Representative's office.

PROFILE

* Working knowledge of legislative committees, constituent relations and the legislative process.
* Experienced in legislative research and in reporting findings necessary to support specific legislation.
* Excellent communication and problem-solving skills.
* Award-winning manager with five years experience in customer relations.

EDUCATION

Masters of Public Affairs, Northwestern University, Evanston, IL (expected 1996)

Bachelor of Science in Management, Cum Laude, University of Illinois, Urbana/Champaign (1991)

WORK EXPERIENCE

Legislative Internship, Illinois House of Representatives, Springfield (January 1995–current)
Work closely on daily basis with state representatives. Handle daily written and verbal contact with constituents. Complete comprehensive research and special projects for representatives. Monitor various committee work and the general session.
* Served on team that researched legislation and conducted meetings with constituents for Senators Duvall and Hudnut regarding Governor Wilson's 1996 budget proposal.
* Presented ideas and research findings, which senators used in legislative session to support proposal, resulting in House approval of the bill.

Blackwell Entertainment Network, Chicago, Ill.
Sales Service Executive (August 1994-December 1994)
Handled national cable schedules on two cable networks. Maintained client and agency relations through written correspondence, phone contact and sales calls. Compiled all needed research. Prepared and presented research materials.
* Recommended and implemented new research tool, which provided more accurate information than current methods and led to increased sales.

(continued)

WORK EXPERIENCE

Blackwell Entertainment Network, Chicago, IL
> **Sales Assistant (May 1993-August 1994)**
> Ordered and serviced client cable schedules. Maintained all inter-company sales/budget figures for Midwest/Chicago area.
> - Consistently received high customer satisfaction ratings and was named Outstanding Sales Assistant for three consecutive months (January-March 1994).

Chicago Tribune, Chicago, IL
> **District Circulation Manager, Elmhurst (March 1992-May 1993)**
> Supervised daily circulation for approximately 12,000 customers. Managed carrier force of nearly 160 independent contractors. Insured proper payment of bills by independent contractors and consumers. Directly supervised two salaried service managers and three part-time district assistants.
> - Developed new incentive program, which increased circulation by rewarding carriers for developing new customers.
> - Named District Manager of the Month (February 1993).

> **Service Manager (June 1991-March 1992)**
> Managed more than 80 carriers serving 4,100 customers. Supervised bill collection, payment and route management.
> - Initiated and implemented new pick-up and loading process, which reduced carriers' waiting time by one hour on weekdays and by two hours on Sunday and resulted in more timely delivery.
> - Promoted to District Circulation Manager after only nine months.

RELATED ACTIVITIES

Election Precinct Judge, Kendall County, IL (1993-1994)
Election Precinct Inspector, Kendall County, IL (1994-1995)
Member, Speaker's Bureau, Illinois Voter Registration Council (1995-current)

PAUL M. VOIGHT
1034 W. Merrick Dr.
Greencastle, IN 46909
(317) 555-8008

OBJECTIVE   A position in warehouse operations management with a large, interstate
retailer or distributor.

SKILLS SUMMARY   Varied but accomplished background in operations, sales and customer
service. Excel in operations management, especially warehouse traffic
management and distribution. Experienced in contracting and scheduling
freight operations. Skilled in reorganizing operations to save money.

EXPERIENCE
Feb 1995-currrent   **Operations Assistant, Replay Records, Indianapolis, IN**
* Assist in managing and supervising central warehouse operations,
  including traffic management and distribution
* Contract, coordinate and schedule freight operations between four stores
* Recommended new handling procedure, which better protects fragile
  warehouse inventory
* Assisted in reorganizing warehouse operations and freight distribution,
  resulting in $75,000 savings annually

Jan 1994-Feb 1995   **Sales Associate, Lewis Jewelers, Greencastle, IN**
* Handled floor sales and assisted customers with purchases
* Designed and implemented new gift registry, which provided computer
  print out of customer's gift list
* Assisted in daily bookkeeping and monthly statements
* Developed special wedding sales promotion, which expanded wedding
  registries by 35%

May 1993-Jan 1994   **Insurance Underwriter, American Insurance Co., Indianapolis, IN**
* Analyzed individual risks for potential liability and property losses
* Communicated verbally and in writing with agents

June 1992-May 1993   **Customer Service Representative, First City Bank, Greencastle, IN**
* Completed daily business transactions, including teller and safe-deposit
  duties
* Assisted in balancing branch's daily books
* Opened new accounts and closed existing accounts
* Recommended new safe-deposit procedure, which reduced paperwork

EDUCATION   DePauw University, Greencastle, IN (1991-1992)
* 21 credit hours in general studies

Mark T. Turner • 233 W. Allen Dr. • Wellington, Pa. • 19032 • (215) 555-8828

Summary of Qualifications

National award-winning sales manager with proven sales and organizational skills. Ability to train and maintain an enthusiastic, productive staff. Excellent experience in account management, reducing projected store losses and exceeding all sales goals.

Work Experience

National Rentals, Inc. (June 1991-current)

Manage sales, rental contracts, repossessions, inventory, and computerized payroll and bookkeeping. Arrange store displays, handle local marketing and advertising. Perform all employee training and evaluation for up to 10 employees.

Store Manager, Wellington, Pa.

(July 1995-current)
- Increased revenues and rental units 25%.
- Named to Star Performers Club, Eastern Division.
- Winner of special incentive contest for unit gain, Eastern Division.
- Named Sales Store of the Month, Eastern Division (October 1995).

Store Manager, Brookville, Ind.

(May 1993-July 1995)
- **Named National Store Manager of the Year for fiscal 1994.**
- Achieved top 1% of sales nationwide.
- Increased revenues and rental units 55%.
- Named Sales Store of the Month, Market 121 (June 1994).
- Reduced projected store losses by 40%.

Store Manager, Wayfare, Ohio

(March 1992-May 1993)
- First account manager to advance to store manager in less than one year.
- Named Sales Store of the Month, all divisions (June and July 1992).
- Achieved fourth place in unit gain for new stores, all divisions (July 1992).
- Earned fourth in store performance income for new stores, all divisions (June 1992).
- Placed second in exceeding plan on average price of rental agreements for new stores, all divisions (June 1992).

Account Manager, Berlington, Mich.

(June 1991-March 1992)
- Initiated new contract review program, which reduced repossessions 25%.
- Eliminated account backlog and computerized all records.

Education

B.S. in Marketing, Southern Michigan University, Sturgis, May 1991

ANNA GILROY
323 South Avon Drive
Milton, NY 10945
(914) 555-2909

OBJECTIVE
A position as a general office clerk for a major corporation.

SKILLS PROFILE
- Ability to operate Lilly 5000 copy/collating machine
- Knowledge and experience with corporate mailroom procedures
- Good filing and organizational skills
- Experience in handling confidential paperwork
- Ability to take accurate phone messages and deliver messages promptly
- Good customer relations background

EMPLOYMENT HISTORY
Copy machine attendant, Hodges, Wilson and Pickard, Milton, NY (1993-current)
- Copy and collate all projects (including confidential papers) for 25-lawyer firm
- Successfully complete all jobs by time requested
- Coordinate delivery of large projects with mailroom clerk
- Initiated "rush procedure," which guarantees "rush" copy projects of 1,000 total pages or less will be completed in 30 minutes of submission; meet all guaranteed deadlines and enhanced copy room operations
- Won the quarterly "Employee Suggestion Award" for "rush procedure"

Mailroom clerk, Hodges, Wilson and Pickard, Milton, NY (1989-1993)
- Accurately filed and delivered mail to all company departments
- Suggested new mail code system, which reduced filing errors and increased timely delivery
- Computed amount of postage required for outgoing mail, depending on weight and classification
- Covered phones for word processing clerk during clerk's lunch break

Waitress/Cashier, The Corner Restaurant, Harris, NY (1987-1989)
- Took orders, served restaurant patrons and assisted at the cash register
- Created "Tuesday Casino Night" theme, including food and games, which doubled the number of customers on a typically slow night

EDUCATION
River Valley High School, Harris, NY (Diploma, 1987)

GLENN T. ROBINSON
55 S. Bailey Ct.
Baton Rouge, LA 70332
(504) 555-6992

OBJECTIVE

A position as a courier.

SKILLS PROFILE

- Excellent driving, safety and attendance record
- Thorough knowledge of area roads, highways and regional airport
- Proven record of completing all deliveries on schedule
- Experienced in operating heavy machinery
- Good background in assembling products and printed materials

EMPLOYMENT HISTORY

Courier, Miller Industries, Baton Rouge, LA (February 1993-October 1995)
- Only driver/courier to log 7,000 miles with no accidents or violations
- Served as liaison and helped develop delivery schedule with new overnight service company located at airport
- Initiated "orange cone" system, which reduced backing accidents in courier group and earned company safety award

Equipment Operator, Street Department, City of Baton Rouge, LA (May 1991-December 1992)
- Worked on city street and bridge repair projects
- Operated heavy machinery, including steam roller and back hoe
- Served on team to evaluate new street cleaning machines; recommended model which reduced work crew time by five hours per week

Assembler, Taylor Printing, Inc., Baton Rouge, LA (February 1989-March 1991)
- Collated and assembled printing projects
- Operated machines that scored and folded brochures

Assembler, Prairie Industries, Baton Rouge, LA. (September 1988-December 1988)
- Produced Christmas garland and trees
- Provided other, general labor in assembly plant for seasonal products

ACTIVITIES

Secretary, Elks Lodge, Baton Rouge

PHYLLIS KRAMER
55 Prairie Lane
Coatsville, ND 58365
(701) 555-3002

OBJECTIVE   A secondary position in biology, general science and/or physical science for grade levels 7 to 12. Looking for the opportunity to generate excitement and interest in the sciences and help junior and senior high school students develop academically, socially and personally.

SKILLS PROFILE
- Experienced in creating lesson plans, designing laboratory experiments and maintaining disciplined atmosphere
- Knowledgeable in designing and evaluating computer science labs
- Strong volunteer/instructional background
- Mature and experienced in working with children of all ages
- Excellent rapport with students
- Skilled in successful fund raising, event planning and program development
- Experienced in Pascal and Basic computer programming

EDUCATION/ ENDORSEMENTS

1995-current	Graduate Studies, North Dakota State University
1985	Endorsements in General Sciences and Physical Sciences, North Dakota State University
1985	B.S. in Biology, *with honors*, North Dakota State University

STUDENT TEACHING

Sept-Dec 1984   **Student Teacher, Marshall High School, Marshall, ND**
- Taught first-year biology and chemistry
- Assisted in second-year biology
- Created a contract system for grades on one unit, resulting in higher achievement and lab and test scores
- Created all daily lessons, tests, laboratory experiments and semester tests for both biology and chemistry

INSTRUCTIONAL EXPERIENCE

1995-current   **Substitute Teacher, Coatsville Jr./Sr. High School, Coatsville, ND**
- Instruct students in all subject areas
- Complete lesson plans as directed and provide teacher with feedback
- Maintain disciplined academic atmosphere

(continued)

INSTRUCTIONAL
EXPERIENCE

1993-current   **Volunteer Science Instructor, Coatsville Community School Corp., Coatsville, ND**
- Assist, instruct and provide feedback to junior- and senior-high school students on a variety of lab projects
- Work with students on defining their research and hypotheses and determining their variables for successful science fair projects

1990-1993   **Church School Teacher/Vacation Bible School Teacher, First United Presbyterian Church, Coatsville, ND**
- Instructed elementary and preschool children each Sunday and during week-long summer Bible school sessions
- Created lesson plans and designed related activities
- Coordinated dramatic presentations for worship services
- Recommended program improvements, which resulted in self-contained learning units and increased church school attendance

1985-1987   **Science Teacher, Prairie Senior High School, Bismarck, ND**
- Taught first-year biology and second-year chemistry students
- Designed special laboratory experiments, which increased interaction and idea-sharing among students
- Coordinated annual science fair and guided students in their research and development of successful projects
- Led committee which designed a state-of-the-art classroom computer lab to provide hands-on learning experiences and better prepare students for higher education

VOLUNTEER/ORGANIZATIONAL
EXPERIENCE

1993-current   **Member, Textbook Adoption Committee, Coatsville Community School System, Coatsville, ND**
- Review elementary-level English, science and mathematics text books and recommend which should be included in curriculum

1994-1995   **Officer, Coatsville Elementary Parent/Teacher Organization, Coatsville, ND**
- Organized most successful fund-raising carnival to date
- Planned and implemented first-ever T-shirt sales program
- Created first-ever Christmas sales program

1993-1994   **Officer, "Ministry of Care," First United Presbyterian Church, Coatsville, ND**
- Created and implemented program to serve church's outreach needs
- Organized volunteers to call on hospital patients and visitors to church
- Developed program to include eight committees and 200 volunteers

Woman with erratic job history due to
husband's relocating
Functional

GRETCHEN MULHONEY

425 E. Kilroy Place • Eastlake, Ohio • 44110 • (216) 555-9223

OBJECTIVE

A position as a business manager for a major retailer.

SKILLS/ABILITIES

Financial

- Skilled in handling credit reporting, collections, bookkeeping and installment contracts for retailer with $3 million in annual sales.
- Experienced in managing collections and developing payment plan programs, which have increased collections by 25%.
- Adept in handling all monthly payments on personal accounts for business owner and balancing all accounts monthly.

Management/Organizational

- Skilled in office management, including accounts payable, accounts receivable, daily and monthly postings, financial statements, monthly and quarterly taxes and payroll for business generating $5 million annually in sales.
- Experienced in managing rental income properties, including collecting rent, depositing and posting income for 60 properties, and paying expenses through eight different accounts.
- Able to train new employees and inform current employees of new policies and procedures and ensure compliance.
- Skilled in developing successful business office procedures, resulting in productive office operations, accurate records and a well-functioning staff.

Communication/Customer Service

- Skilled in providing information and counseling bank customers on account services that would best serve their needs.
- Experienced in initiating special services for car repair customers, resulting in increased customer satisfaction and increased return business.

WORK EXPERIENCE

Business Manager, Anderson Ford, Eastlake, Ohio (1993-present)
Business Manager, Kessler Chevrolet, Flint, Mich. (1990-1993)
Office Manager, Meyers Furniture, Merrillville, Ind. (1986-1990)
Savings Department Supervisor, Union National Bank, Lansing, Ill. (1983-1986)
Teller, Wisconsin State Bank, Whitewater, Wis. (1980-1983)

EDUCATION

Associate's Degree in Supervision, Illinois University (1986)
Financial Courses, American Institute of Banking (1983-1985)

HONORS

Business Managers Award from district office (1991, 1992, 1994, 1995)

Woman transferring volunteer
experience into work skills
Functional

ANNE K. JOHNSON

501 Brenden Way • Twinsburg, IN • 46269 • (219) 555-1924

OBJECTIVE

A position as a fund raiser/volunteer organizer for a nonprofit organization.

SKILLS/ABILITIES

Management/Organization

- Coordinated philanthropic organization's "Tour of Homes" fund raiser for three years, raising $3,600 the first year, $4,200 the second year and $5,300 the third year.
- Served two terms as president of philanthropic group; increased membership 30%; established new fund raiser that brought in $1,500 annually to benefit the community.
- Recruited and organized for four years up to 40 volunteers for church's annual summer vacation Bible school.
- Served as secretary for school Parent/Teacher Organization for two years.
- Chaired and organized PTO school carnival which raised $2,500 and was the most successful fund-raising event in 10 years.
- Assisted in coordinating volunteer drivers for senior services organization.

Teaching/Training

- Planned curriculum for vacation Bible school for two years.
- Planned curriculum and taught preschool and kindergarten Sunday School classes for three years.
- Tutored (through library program) four first- and second-grade students in reading.
- Hosted story hour with children's librarian at local public library, including scheduling special guests and organizing visits to the police and fire departments, post office and more.

Communication/Leadership

- Developed and distributed brochures for local public library about children's programs, which nearly doubled attendance at the programs.
- Helped create brochure explaining local, state and federal services and funds for food and child care assistance for low-income families.
- Served on team with representatives from county agencies to develop and implement child care provider training and certification program to improve the quality of child care offered in private homes.

VOLUNTEER WORK HISTORY

Twinsburg Public Library, Children's Department, Tutoring Department, Twinsburg, IN (1992-current)
Twinsburg Christian Church, Children's Education Department, Twinsburg, IN (1991-current)
Twinsburg Public Schools, Parent/Teacher Organization, Twinsburg, IN (1994-current)
Psi Iota Xi national philanthropic sorority, Omega Chapter, Twinsburg, IN (1987-current)
Greensboro County Senior Services, Volunteer Transportation (1993-current)
Greensboro County Youth Action Coalition, Child Care Services Team, Twinsburg, IN (1995-current)

EDUCATION

Bachelor of Arts in Consumer and Family Sciences, Indiana State University, Terre Haute (1985)

MICHELLE R. HAUGHTON
33 Lakeview Dr.
Hunter Lake, MN 56453
(218) 555-2993

OBJECTIVE   A supervisory position in project management.

PROFILE   Six years engineering, design, processing and development experience in the automotive industry. Skilled in working with team to design and develop innovative advance engine products. Hold two patents.

SKILLS/ABILITIES

Design
- Served on team that designed and developed innovative automotive engine project from concept layout through vehicle testing on three engine phases.
- Experienced with finite element, thermodynamic modeling, design verification, failure mode effects analysis, design for manufacture and assembly.
- Able to incorporate combustion knowledge into base engine design.

Development
- Developed bench and dynamometer test plans for engines and components.
- Use rapid prototype techniques to save material budget and time.
- Apply statistical techniques to develop and design experiments.

Process
- Designed parts for all major casting techniques in ferrous and non-ferrous alloys.
- Experienced with high- and low-volume machining processes, including geometric tolerances.

EMPLOYMENT HISTORY

Glasgow Motor Corporation, St. Paul, MN
- Product Engineer (1991-current)
- Cooperative Education Student, Product Development (1989-1991)

EDUCATION

Master of Science in Mechanical Engineering, University of Minnesota (expected 1997)

Bachelor of Science in Mechanical Engineering, University of Minnesota (1991)

Nancy Gilson
4665 S 250 W
North Platte, Ind. 41004
(219) 555-9293

Career goal   A position as a food services manager or catering supervisor.

Summary of experience

Organizational/management skills
- Organize, host, plan menu and supervise preparation of all food for 500 guests at annual Indiana Cattle Association picnic (23 years).
- Plan and organize annual State Fair picnic for more than 400 cattle owners and guests, including securing sponsorships and donations of soft drinks, paper and plastic goods (12 years).
- Organize up to 120 volunteers and supervise food preparation and forecasting for State Fair beef tent, which brings in $100,000 annually for the state cattle association (10 years).
- Organize and supervise up to 25 volunteers for church's annual fall craft fair/luncheon; have successfully planned and met budget for 11 years and raised more than $7,000 for church and charitable causes.
- Planned, purchased goods, organized up to 10 volunteers and helped prepare nutritious snacks for weekly church school classes (7 years).
- Chair meal portion of home economic club's annual fall bazaar and luncheon, including purchasing goods and supervising food preparation; for 8 years have consistently brought food purchases in under budget and exceeded fund-raising goals by 20%.

Financial/budgeting skills
- Skilled in handling computerized bookkeeping for 1,200-acre grain and 250-head cattle farming operation.
- Initiated and completed data entry from manual to computerized record-keeping system, resulting in improved account analysis, improved report generation for loan/banking and tax purposes, and reduced bookkeeping time.
- Experienced in monthly farm and household budgeting and timely payment of personal and business accounts.

Other related skills
- Experienced in planning and creating low-fat, low-sugar and low-sodium meals.
- Skilled in presenting knowledgeable instruction on proper food handling and storage.

Education   Bachelor of Science in Home Economics, Purdue University, West Lafayette, Ind.

Memberships   President, Secretary, Treasurer, Out and About Home Ec Club, Warren County, Ind.
President, Treasurer, United Methodist Women, United Methodist Church, North Platte, Ind.

Marcia T. Gestault
105 S. Esplanade Dr.
Greenville, Mich. 49002
(313) 555-3203

Career objective   To secure a position in collegiate student affairs, involving program development, advisory and/or communication responsibilities.

Summary of qualifications

Advisory skills

- Advised Student Activities Program Board at community college, including contract negotiation, planning, event implementation, technical production, budgeting, critical thinking, ethics and communication.
- Advised Greek council, a Panhellenic council and members of five social fraternities and sororities in urban commuter university.
- Disciplined fraternities and sororities in accordance with university policies and procedures.
- Coordinated development of a university Panhellenic council.

Communication skills

- Prepared annual reports pertaining to positions held in higher education and private sector.
- Developed, administered and interpreted results of annual commencement survey directed to more than 600 graduates.
- Developed, administered and interpreted results of survey directed to 166 student organization presidents regarding leadership perceptions.
- Presented educational workshops on local, regional and national levels to audiences of up to 150.

Program development
skills

- Coordinated and managed all aspects of more than 40 events sponsored by Student Activities Program Board.
- Organized structured training program related to all aspects of planning and executing events.
- Presented educational sessions relating to programming at regional conferences of the National Association for Campus Activities.
- Coordinated leadership seminars involving up to 70 students.
- Created special programs for fraternities and sororities based on chapter needs.

(continued)

Summary of qualifications

Management skills
- Managed budget of more than $150,000 and maintained accounts for commencement, program board and capital outlays.
- Directed two chapter colonizations of social Greek organizations, including scheduling, advertising, recruiting student assistants and public relations; increased membership 40% among organizations.
- Revised university policies concerning legal/fiscal relationships with Greek organizations.
- Hired, trained and supervised staff of 12 student workers and two clerical staff.
- Assisted in developing student activities mission statement at two institutions.

Editing skills
- Produced membership newsletter six times annually for 2,000 members of national professional fraternity.
- Prepared information packets for 34 student chapters, 41 chapter advisors, 12 alumni chapters, eight regional officers and 10 national officers each quarter.
- Created and revised fraternity publications and manuals.

Employment history

Program Manager, College of Royal Oak, Royal Oak, Mich. (1986-1990)
Coordinator of Student Affairs, Madison College, Madison, Wis. (1981-1986)
Greek Advisor, University of Wisconsin at Milwaukee, Wis. (1980-1981)
Secondary Teacher, Indianapolis Public School System, Indianapolis, Ind. (1958-1979)

Education

Master's Degree in College Student Personnel Administration, University of Wisconsin at Milwaukee, with highest honors (1981)
Bachelor's Degree in Education, Indiana University, Bloomington (1958)

Activities

Planning Committee, Fall Harvest Festival, Greenville, Mich. (1990-current)
Volunteer, Parkwood Nursing Home, Royal Oak, Mich. (1991-current)

Mason J. Wheeler

855 Princeton Place
Wanatah, MN 55776
(218) 555-9223

Objective

A position as an insurance agent.

Summary of Skills

- Licensed insurance agent in life, health and casualty
- Experienced in working with insurance companies to develop employee benefit plans
- Nearly 20 years management experience in private and public sector
- Excellent interpersonal skills

Work Experience

Deputy Director, Minnesota Emergency Medical Services Commission, Minneapolis, MN
(May 1990-current)
Manage and supervise office and field staff of 17. Maintain liaison with regional, state and national agencies and organizations. Direct all agency programs and investigations.
- Administer state and federal grants and assist in preparing and managing agency budget
- Consult with variety of insurance companies to enhance employee benefit plans
- Established and implemented EMS regional coordination and quality assurance system, which raised standards of service provided
- Developed Advanced Life Support Planning and Implementation Manual, which standardized procedures and equipment levels across the state

Transportation Director, Minnesota Emergency Medical Services Commission, Minneapolis, MN
(September 1987-May 1990)
Administered transportation and disaster component of emergency medical services in State of Minnesota.
- Evaluated and approved all emergency medical services providers and vehicles for state certification
- Developed regional emergency medical services, systems, transportation and disaster plans
- Established Air Ambulance Standards for statewide implementation

Administrative Assistant, Decatur County Memorial Hospital, Wanatah, MN
(January 1984-September 1987)
Handled general administration. Wrote grants and proposals.
- Directed Decatur County Emergency Medical Services
- Assisted with event planning, public relations and special projects

(continued)

Work Experience

Director of Decatur County Emergency Medical Services, Board of Commissioners of Decatur County, Wanatah, MN

(October 1981-January 1984)

Administered county emergency medical services. Trained, supervised and hired/fired staff of 11 full-time (paid) and 60 part-time (volunteers) employees.

- Supervised maintenance of all ambulances in three county locations
- Purchased materials and administered Medicare/Medicaid accounts
- Handled budgeting, planning, public relations and in-service/training activities

Commissioner's Administrative Assistant, Decatur County Board of Commissioners, Wanatah, MN

(August 1977-October 1981)

- Served as liaison to board and county offices
- Wrote and processed federal and state grants, loans and policy proposals
- Conducted computer study for county ambulance service and supervised conversion to computerized records

Education/Licensing/Certification

Licensed Insurance Agent (1994)

M.S. in Public Administration, Minnesota University School of Public and Environmental Affairs, Lakeland, MN (1980)

Certified Emergency Medical Technician (since 1958)

B.S. in Business Administration, Minnesota University, Lakeland, MN (1957)

Activities

Director, Decatur County Parks & Recreation Board
Member, Decatur County Economic Development Planning Commission

Older male with management
experience recently laid off
Chronological

Anthony Salvatore
458 E. Salisbury Lane
Willow, NY 10967
(914) 555-6768

Skills Summary

Senior manager with extensive experience in site development. Skilled in securing federal, state and local regulatory land-use approvals. Excellent background in facility design, construction, scheduling and budgeting. Experienced in developing and implementing regional and nationwide renovation programs for major organizations.

Employment

Senior Manager-Site Development, Truman & Associates, Inc., Willow, NY (May 1985-October 1995)
- Managed due diligence requirements and governmental land-use approvals throughout the eastern United States for one of company's top accounts.
- Handled site selection and layout, defined design criteria, completed initial planning and cost estimates and secured funds.
- Coordinated and obtained all federal, state and local regulatory land-use approvals.
- Interfaced with local planning, operating, finance and legal organizations to meet local requirements and create positive relationship with community and civic leaders.
- Negotiated real estate documents and consultant contracts.

Senior Architectural Project Manager, Dothby's, Inc., Garden City, NJ (March 1978-May 1985)
- Handled complete design and construction coordination of company's retail facilities throughout the Northeastern United States and Atlantic Seaboard.
- Developed and implemented a nationwide remodel program for existing stores, which enhanced store operations, stock organization and overall appearance.

Project Engineer, Corporate Real Estate Management, Atlantic Telephone & Electronics, Washington, DC (October 1973-March 1978)
- Managed design and construction of new buildings and renovations for office and equipment space at headquarters and in the field.
- Supervised and completed more than 40 projects in less than five years.
- Recommended and implemented new switching center design, which resulted in improved equipment maintenance and switching operations.

Facilities Design Engineer, Corporate Real Estate Management, Atlantic Telephone & Electronics, Washington, DC (June 1963-October 1973)
- Designed and provided cost estimates for new facilities.
- Recommended and implemented renovations program for out-of-date facilities, saving $20 million in new building costs.

Education

B.S. Civil Engineering, Pennsylvania State University

Individual who hasn't worked
for a while
Functional

Deborah K. Lyons
155 W. Tamarack Dr.
Batesville, Ark. 72502
(501) 555-9293

Career goal   A community relations position.

Summary of experience

Organizational/management skills
- Organized volunteers, secured corporate donations and planned fund-raising events to pay for construction of $2 million Boys' and Girls' Club facility.
- Serve on board of directors for club, help develop policies and procedures and coordinate annual fund-raising auction, which provides more than $6,500 for operational expenses.
- Recruited to supervise annual fund and membership drive for local library, raising donations 35% and membership 20% in two years.
- Served two terms as secretary/treasurer of Parent/Teacher Association and recommended new parent/teacher conference idea that increased parent classroom participation 35%.
- Managed three-member staff at rehabilitation hospital and increased productivity 25% despite operational changes brought on by two new owners in five years.

Communication/marketing skills
- Work with local businesses and civic organizations to gain sponsors for 30 soccer, 40 basketball and 25 baseball teams.
- Developed brochure to attract and retain club members and sponsors.
- Handle publicity for local March of Dimes walk-a-thon, which has seen participation increase 35% and donations increase 40% over the last three years.
- Handled three in-house, high-volume accounts for rehabilitation hospital and helped develop long-term marketing plan that increased number of clients 25%.

Instructional skills
- Supervised Arkansas Dyslexic Association's Saturday math program for more than 300 students and tutored up to 30 hours per week.
- Developed new tour guide program for local hospital and trained up to 15 volunteer tour guides.

Experience   Fund-raising Chairperson, Batesville Public Library (1994-current)
Director, Fund-raising Chairperson, Batesville Boys' and Girls' Club (1992-current)
Local Publicity Chairman, March of Dimes Walk-a-thon (1992-current)
Volunteer, Wishard Memorial Hospital, Batesville, Ark. (1991-1992)
Secretary/Treasurer, Parent/Teacher Association, Tipton County Community
    School Corp. (1989-1991)
Volunteer, Arkansas Dyslexic Association, Little Rock (1988-1991)
Admissions Director, McKenzie Hospitals, Little Rock (1983-1988)
LPN, McKenzie Hospitals, Little Rock (1981-1983)
LPN, Robert W. Hall, M.D., Batesville (1980-1981)

Military entering civilian work force
(into a different field)
Chronological

SANDRA W. RICHARDSON
39 Citation Circle
Ames, Iowa 50602
(319) 555-6887

CAREER OBJECTIVE

A position as a secondary teacher.

SKILLS SUMMARY

Manager, engineer and instructor with extensive background in operations, leadership, instruction and training. Demonstrated ability to successfully train and lead up to 1,800-person unit. Solid education in instructional techniques. Licensed teacher in the state of Iowa.

EDUCATION

Iowa State University, Ames, Iowa (1993-1995)
• Undergraduate courses to fulfill teaching certificate requirements

U.S. Military Academy, West Point, NY (1984)
• Bachelor of Science in Engineering

PROFESSIONAL STUDIES

Officer Basic and Advanced Course (1986)
• 18-month post-graduate schooling that included lesson plan preparation, instruction and training techniques

Combined Arms Staff College (1987)
• Senior officer schooling focusing on staff and administrative functions and covering advanced briefing and instructional techniques

LICENSING

Secondary Education Teaching Certificate - State of Iowa (1995)

INSTRUCTIONAL EXPERIENCE
1995-current

Substitute Teacher, Ames Public School System, Ames, Iowa
Complete a variety of assignments, including 12-week assignment in high school biology and chemistry classes.
• Created special unit for history curriculum on Desert Storm and its significance in U.S. military history

(continued)

**INSTRUCTIONAL
EXPERIENCE**

1990-1992   **Operations Manager, U.S. Army, Dhahran, Saudi Arabia**
Handled all operations and training of 1,800-person logistics unit that
provided supplies for Middle East. Tour of duty included Operation
Desert Storm.
- Unit commended by General Schwartzkopf
- Demonstrated ability to rapidly create and execute team training
  program under demanding conditions

1989-1990   **Commander, U.S. Army, West Germany**
Managed 150-person unit.
- Administered training program that effectively taught individual,
  collective and multi-echelon (various level of command) skills to
  produce a combat-ready unit.

1985-1989   **Training Officer, U.S. Army, California and West Germany**
Served as training supervisor for 125-person unit and training manager
for 500-person unit.
- Handled hands-on teaching and curriculum development
- Created alternative means of assessment, which more accurately
  identified accomplishments and areas needing improvement

1984   **Cadet Basic Training Squad Leader and Platoon Leader, U.S.
Military Academy, West Point, NY**
Taught and led unique and exciting eight-week educational experience.
- Served on team that transformed a culturally and educationally
  diverse freshman class into a cohesive group of young men and
  women, prepared for rigors of cadet life.

ACTIVITIES   Volunteer Tutor, Carnegie Public Library, Ames, Iowa
Girl Scout Leader, Troop 121, Ames, Iowa

EDWARD T. FIELDS
105 Magnolia Dr.
Talagusa, FL 32302
(904) 555-1664

Skills Profile

Nearly 10 years aeronautical and engineering experience, including obtaining five commercial and experimental patents. Skilled in developing methods that have become·Air Force standards. Solid background in computer and software operations, budget and personnel management, and training.

Work Experience

Aug 1992-current

Air Force Flight Test Center, Samuels Air Force Base, FL
Captain/Flight Commander
Program manager for testing and evaluating integrated software systems on F-15 aircraft. F-15 airborne test director and weapon system operator.
- Managed schedule and costs within budget of approximately $14M per year.
- Supervised 17 engineers and three technicians, wrote performance evaluations and oversaw training.
- Saved $120K in annual costs through cross-training.
- Developed original methods for weapons accuracy analysis, which was published and presented at professional conference and recommended for Air Force standard.

May 1991-Aug 1992

Air Force Flight Test Center, Samuels Air Force Base, FL
Captain/Lead Avionics Engineer
Prepared technical and safety flight test plans, reviewed and approved technical reports of test results and authorized specific flight profiles.
- Directed hazardous, low-level flight program with no safety incidents.
- Wrote published standards of radar altimeter suitability as test data source.
- Implemented computerized data base to control aircraft software configuration.

June 1986-Aug 1988

Shuttle Test Group, Williams Air Force Base, CA
Lieutenant/Mechanisms Engineer
Served with unit providing Air Force support for Space Shuttle operations.
- Console-certified engineer for pre-launch processing and launch operations.
- Member of Kennedy Space Center launch control room team for four launches.

(continued)

Education

United States Air Force Test Pilot School, Williams Air Force Base, CA (1991)

Air Force Institute of Technology, Dayton, OH (1990)
* Masters of Science in Aeronautical Engineering
* Awarded joint patent on experimental nozzle design

Syracuse University, Syracuse, New York (1986)
* Bachelor of Arts in Engineering Science
* Received joint patent on commercial electro-mechanical design

Current Status

Captain, United States Air Force Reserve (Clearance: Secret)

Awards

Meritorious Service Medal for Operation Desert Storm deployment
1994 Outstanding Volunteer, Talagusa Girls' and Boys' Club

Activities

Volunteer/Basketball Coach, Talagusa Girls' and Boys' Club (1993-current)
Project Leader, Eagle Scout Radio-Controlled Airplane project (1993-current)

Linda T. Gillespie
901 S. Hemingway
Millwood, NY 10531
(914) 555-2232

PROFESSIONAL PROFILE Published software professional with expertise in automatic English analysis, including text critiquing, text abstracting and multimedia retrieval. Strong background in applied research and linguistics. Excellent programming skills. Software patent pending.

PROFESSIONAL EXPERIENCE

1994-present **Consultant, It's Academic Inc., New York City, NY**

- Provide specialized consultation in automatic language analysis.
- Create programs for Microsoft Corporation, Educational Testing Service and Columbia University.
- Developed an ambiguity resolution component for Microsoft, which selects appropriate senses for words that have multiple meanings.

1989-1994 **Staff Programmer, Artificial Intelligence Department, FBP Corporation, Williams Research Center, Rochester, NY**

Object-oriented Graphical Abstractor (1992-1994)
- Developed user interface issues related to displaying document abstracts graphically.
- Addressed issues of displaying and traversing graphical networks.

Multimedia Indexor (1991-1992)
- Enhanced retrieval of multi-media objects described by indexes.
- Developed dictionary relationships (synonym and taxonym), which expanded user queries to include related items.

Grammar and Style Checker (1989-1991)
- Served as member of critique team, which did pioneering work in writer's tools by developing the first tool based on a full syntactic parse.
- Handled user interface and performance issues including:
  - Incorporating suggested corrections into a text editor
  - Supporting interactive changes to the text
  - Enhancing servers to distribute CPU-intensive processing across platforms and to handle multiple users
  - Creating user profiles to allow users to specify personal preferences for style checking

(continued)

PROFESSIONAL EXPERIENCE

1985-1989   **Senior Associate Programmer, Documentation Automaton Systems, FBP Corporation, Federal Systems Division, Hopewell, VA**

- Developed documentation automation system to reduce production costs of documentation, resulting in $1.6M savings during the first four years.
- Negotiated an agreement for software to ensure compliance with U.S. military readability requirements, resulting in a $1.1M savings.

LANGUAGES/ ENVIRONMENTS   C, Smalltalk, C++, PL1, REXX, Pascal, Windows, VM/CMS

EDUCATION   MS in Computer Science, New York University (1992)
BS in Computer Science, The Ohio State University (1985)

PUBLICATIONS   Gillespie, "Sense Disambiguation Using On-Line Dictionaries," *Natural Language Processing*, Academic Publishers, Inc., 1993.

Barker, Gillespie, McFry, "Post-Recognizer Processing: Applications for Automatic Speech," *Signal Processing Conference,* 1991.

Gillespie and Knight, "Lexicons for Broad Coverage Semantics," *Lexical Acquisitions,* Davis Associates Publishers, 1990.

Davis and Gillespie, "The Experience of Developing a Large-Scale Natural Language Text Processing System," *Conference on Applied Natural Language Processing,* 1989.

PATENTS   Patent pending for *A Method for Indexing of Multimedia Objects*

AWARDS   Outstanding Technical Achievement Award, FBP Corporation (1989)
Outstanding Research Contributions Award, FBP Corporation (1992, 1993)

ACTIVITIES   Local Walk Coordinator, March of Dimes, Millwood, NY (1992-current)

Marissa Handlon
35 West Parker Way
Henderson, NJ 07553
(201) 555-5039

SKILLS SUMMARY   Software and hardware expert with more than 10 years of experience in project planning and management, program management and systems integration. Strong background in telecommunications applications. Experienced in integrating internal computer services and needs into the business planning process. Skilled in training and team building, including identifying problems and designing solutions. Adept at working with interdependent departments and organizations to develop and implement program plans.

EDUCATION   MBA, Marketing/Finance, Northwestern University (1992)
BS, Computer Science, Michigan State University (1986)

WORK EXPERIENCE

Technical Director, Public Communications, Atlantic Tel, Rochester, NJ   **1993-current**
Manage operations of software development and maintenance team.

- Developed and started three-year plan to consolidate and upgrade obsolete UNIX minicomputer hardware and convert mission critical production software to the new platform.
- Managed the hardware and network procurement and installation across several business units, assessing and redesigning existing production systems to better fit changing business needs.
- Restructured software development team to increase productivity and build individual technical skills.
- Implemented a quarterly performance feedback process and reinforced basic project management processes.
- Addressed chronic maintenance problems and increasing internal user demand for services by actively working with senior management to highlight technical issues.
- Results of analysis included funding for a disaster planning project, implementation of a PC-based application for finance group to demonstrate end-user computing, and creation of a systems support team as a member of the annual business planning process.

(continued)

WORK EXPERIENCE

Senior Manager, Davis Consulting, Chicago, IL   **1986-1993**
Managed small- to large-systems projects, from proposal to full implementation.

Project Planning and Management
Regional Telephone Company

- Developed multi-year project phasing strategy across several interdependent organizations to achieve benefits as early as possible by identifying palatable phasing strategies, negotiating with individual projects to determine feasibility, identifying dependencies and developing action plan.
- Supervised the development of the conversion plan, including preparing the technical design, estimating the detail design and manual conversion efforts, developing the master conversion schedule to match a phased implementation and obtaining approval from affected departments.
- Managed the development of field support software for sales representatives and developed opportunity to jointly market the software to other local exchange carriers.

Project Management
Large Personal Computer Manufacturer

- Achieved management consensus on action plan for funds and commissions project by defining feasible alternatives, negotiating approach across several internal organizations and gaining approval for implementation tasks.
- Completed requirements phase, including documenting key features and functions, reviewing and obtaining approval of documentation and defining an implementation approach.

Systems Integration
County Human Services Agency

- Managed the technical architecture team that designed and developed the county's expert system/workstation-based welfare eligibility system and determined the feasibility of the multi-vendor hardware/software solution.
- Successfully developed and managed complex implementation schedule which incorporated procuring $3.5M in hardware and software, selecting a site preparation vendor, installing a 350-workstation network across three sites, coordinating mainframe installation and training 350 users.

ACTIVITIES   Secretary, Michigan State University Alumnae, New Jersey Chapter
Volunteer/Computer Operations Advisor, Henderson Boys' and Girls' Club

Occupational resumes

GWEN H. INGRAM
438 South Street
Camden, Utah 84776
(801) 555-2242

SKILLS SUMMARY

Certified Public Accountant with seven years experience, specializing in cost accounting. Skilled in analyzing data, performing audits and examining internal control procedures. Solid background in, and knowledge of, financial accounting systems.

COMPUTER SKILLS

Lotus, Excel, Ami Pro, WordPerfect, ProComm Plus, Spreadsheet Auditor, Flowcharting III and Focaudit

ACCOUNTING EXPERIENCE

June 1993-current

Senior Accountant/Analyst
Western Mutual - Medicare
Salt Lake City, Utah

Determine reimbursable costs payable to providers of medical care under the Medicare program.
- Analyze financial and statistical data submitted on provider cost reports.
- Review current and fixed assets, liabilities, charges, revenue and expenses.
- Compile statistical data for the basis of allocation of indirect costs.
- Prepare audit adjustment reports.
- Initiated and implemented new provider pricing policies, which established consistency in charges.

Aug 1989-June 1993

Staff Auditor - Corporate Trust, Operations and Retail Lending
First Bank and Trust
Salt Lake City, Utah

Performed financial, operational, regulatory compliance and system-integrated audits. Trained and supervised work of assigned staff.
- Conducted examinations of internal control procedures, which led to improved financial accounting operations.
- Prepared audit reports and developed recommendations for bank officers and bank management.
- Assisted in pre-acquisition audits of purchased banks to determine financial condition, leading to successful business expansion.

(continued)

OTHER EXPERIENCE

Feb 1988-Aug 1989   **Loan Officer**
Citizens Trust
Camden, Utah

Developed, originated, documented and closed commercial, consumer and mortgage loans, concentrating in residential construction lending.
- Served on team that developed and implemented new policies and procedures involving commercial lending, resulting in higher customer satisfaction.
- Developed and implemented indirect lending program, which filled a need as identified by customer feedback.

June 1986-Feb 1988   **Loan Processor**
Citizens Trust
Camden, Utah

Assisted loan officer in documenting and closing commercial, consumer and mortgage loans.
- Member of team that doubled mortgage turnover in two years.

EDUCATION

University of Utah, Salt Lake City
- 12 credit hours in Continuing Education in Accounting (1992-1993)
- Bachelor of Science in Business Administration (1986)

LICENSING

Certified Public Accountant (1989)

ACTIVITIES

Member, Camden Community Band
Planning Committe, Camden Fourth of July Festival
Treasurer, Kappa Kappa Kappa philanthropic organization

MONICA HARRISON
101 Sonnet Lane
Eagleton, WA 99002
(509) 555-7209

SUMMARY OF QUALIFICATIONS

- More than 10 years of tax and accounting research and experience.
- Thorough knowledge of all types of taxes and tax and financial issues.
- Experienced in establishing corporate tax department and 401k plan.
- Skilled in preparing corporate and personal tax returns, with specialized background in pension plans, not-for-profit organizations, farms and consolidated, multi-state corporate returns.
- Strong administrative experience.

PROFESSIONAL EXPERIENCE

March 1992-present

Tax Manager, American North Airlines, Seattle, WA
Administer all functions relating to federal, state and local income, excise, property and transaction taxes, as well as foreign value-added taxes.
Review and assist in preparing all tax accruals and tax account balance sheet reconciliations. Review all payroll tax returns.
- Identify and analyze the tax effects of all company transactions, including the establishment and purchase of subsidiaries, ensuring positive business decisions.
- Recommend necessary changes in internal procedures to comply with tax law changes.
- Provide guidance to the Human Resources Department with respect to fringe benefits, including 401k plan.
- Helped develop and implement "cafeteria-style" benefits plan, which provides employees with a variety of benefits and enhances the company's benefits package.

November 1990-March 1992

Tax Staff Accountant, American North Airlines, Seattle, WA
- Developed a tax department for the company, including completing research and developing all tax functions, resulting in substantial annual savings previously paid to an outside tax consulting firm.
- Established a 401k plan for company employees, enhancing the company's benefit package.
- Performed non-tax-related duties, such as compiling projections and helping analyze financial decisions.

(continued)

PROFESSIONAL EXPERIENCE

May 1987-November 1990

Tax Senior, Whitlatch and Henry, Seattle, WA
- Prepared and reviewed individual, partnership and corporate returns, including consolidated and multi-state corporate returns.
- Specialized in research, compilation of financial projections, business valuations and interstate taxation (income and transaction taxes).
- Trained other staff tax preparers on new computer software, saving $4,500 in outside training costs.

January 1986-May 1987

Tax Senior, Turner McDonald & Co., San Diego, CA
- Supervised and trained newer staff members.
- Specialized in pension plans, not-for-profit organizations, farms and consolidated, multi-state corporate returns.
- Recommended new computer software which reduced manual computation time and increased productivity.

March 1985-January 1986

Staff Accountant, Turner McDonald & Co., San Diego, CA
- Prepared various tax returns and researched tax issues.
- Revised intern program, resulting in increased productivity for company and broader experience for interns.

January 1984-April 1984

Audit Intern, Turner McDonald & Co., San Diego, CA
- Assisted with four audits and performed a complete audit of a political action committee.

EDUCATION

1984

University of Northern California, San Diego
Bachelor of Science in Accounting

PROFESSIONAL AFFILIATIONS

1990-present **Tax Executives Institute**
1994-1995 - Chapter Director
1993-1994 - Membership Committee Chairperson
1993-present **Northwest CPA Society**
1995 - Regional Representative
1994-present **National Tax Accountants Network**

RELATED VOLUNTEER WORK

1993-present Senior Services Center, Eagleton, WA
- Provide tax preparation and tax consulting for senior citizens
1991-1993 First Christian Church
- Treasurer

Thomas K. Eden
32 S. Riverview
Ogden, Iowa 50113
(515) 555-7998

Profile:

Award-winning writer and editor with extensive corporate communications background. Adept in developing and implementing communication plans and programs related to company consolidations. Good background in speech writing, media relations and community events planning. Skilled in desktop publishing.

Work Experience:

Jan 1990 - current

Manager-Employee Communications, Nova TeleCommunications Co., Benton, Iowa (formerly General Telephone Co.)
Prepare, plan and organize information communicated to company's 15,000 employees. Produce six publications designed to maintain and enhance employee morale, perception and understanding of company missions.
- Initiated, researched and developed comprehensive employee communications program redesign (including employee focus groups), which became the model for the new corporate headquarters.
- Developed and implemented communications plans for consolidating 17 operator service offices to 4, and 33 customer contact offices to 10, which helped employee transition to–and understanding of–centralized operations.
- Revised publication production schedule and method to decrease publication costs by 30%.
- Recommended cost-cutting measures for annual executive conference, which reduced expenses by $17,000.
- Produced award-winning publications.

March 1988 - Jan 1990

Administrator-External Communications, General Telephone Co., Benton, Iowa
Handled media relations and served as spokesperson for regional headquarters. Wrote all news releases and submitted headquarters-based news releases to state offices to be tailored for local use.
- Researched and wrote monthly bill insert covering customer, deregulation and general-interest information.
- Established "hometown feature" program, releasing company newspaper articles to employee's local newspapers, enhancing the company's image in its communities.

(continued)

118

Work Experience:

March 1988 - Jan 1990 — **Administrator-External Communications, General Telephone Co., Benton, Iowa**
- Reorganized monthly meeting schedule with state staffs to save department $4,500 monthly.
- Developed and implemented community relations/corporate-giving program, which donated more than $10,000 to local organizations based on employee involvement.

May 1986 - March 1988 — **Employee Communications Administrator, Waldrop Corporation, Iowa City, Iowa**
Prepared, edited and distributed information to 5,000 employees in three states. Developed strike communication plan.
- Wrote, organized and compiled "briefing book," including company, geographical, governmental, economic and community information for use with visiting executives.
- Investigated and established electronic mail procedures, which enhanced timely communication to employees and basically eliminated paper and printing costs.
- Inherited struggling management publication and made it an award-winning piece.
- Managed informal communications program where executives met with groups of employees over breakfast; survey results revealed increased trust among employees with company executives.

Nov 1980 - May 1986 — **Assistant Editor, *Daily Times*, Flora, Iowa**
Began career as reporter for daily city newspaper, circulation 7,500. Promoted to city editor after three years and became assistant editor in November 1985.
- Implemented desktop publishing system and new printing equipment which significantly reduced production costs and speeded production by 45%.
- Worked with advertising team to expand number of advertisers and develop special advertising promotions; increased advertising budget 30%.

Education:

Indiana University, Bloomington, Indiana
Bachelor of Arts in Journalism (1979)

Achievements/Honors:

IABC (International Association of Business Communicators) EPIC (Excellent Performance in Communication) Award--First Place, News/Magapaper (1992, 1993)
IABC EPIC Award–First Place, Employee Newsletter (1991, 1993)
IABC EPIC Award–First Place, Management Publication (1990)

TIM G. COLEMAN

821 Jackson St., Apt. 21B   (215) 555-0220
Philadelphia, PA 19021

SUMMARY OF SKILLS

Award-winning graphic artist with extensive experience in state-of-the-art technologies. Skilled in creating and successfully implementing new product lines to compete with market leaders. Also skilled in video production and computer-generated images, including creating two- and three-dimensional programs and commercials.

PROGRAMS AND SYSTEMS

- Macintosh and IBM systems
- CorelDraw! and Aldus PageMaker on IBM
- Adobe Photoshop, Adobe Illustrator, Aldus Freehand, Adobe Premier, Macromind Director, StrataVision 3-D, Strata Studio Pro on Macintosh
- Commadore Amiga 4000 computer system running with "Video Toaster"
- 3-D animation using Lightwave 3-D
- 2-D animation using Brilliance

WORK EXPERIENCE

June 1994-current

Video Graphic Artist, Showtime Productions, Titus, PA
- Create and edit short animation sequences for use in commercial and private video production.
- Alter still video pictures for use in broadcast video.
- Complete linear editing for a variety of projects.
- Researched and implemented use of Adobe Premier, which provides client with a non-linear hard copy of a planned commercial before investing expensive production time, resulting in substantial savings for the client and the company.
- Created and produced 15 commercials and five short animation sequences in one year on part-time basis.

(continued)

WORK EXPERIENCE

March 1993-current
Graphic Artist, National Card Co., Philadelphia, PA
- Create designs and lettering for greeting cards, gift wraps, gift boxes, party goods and accessories using Adobe Illustrator, Aldus Freehand, QuarkXPress and Adobe Photoshop.
- Coordinate production of all items.
- Designed new children's humorous greeting card and gift wrap line, which increased sales in that area by 45%.
- Recommended and worked with sales representatives to introduce new line of coordinated party items, which successfully competes with current market leader.
- Created and currently coordinating production of new holiday gift wrap design.

June 1991-March 1993
Graphic Artist, Creative Graphics, Willow, PA
- Completed design work for a free-lance design group specializing in concept, layout and production of original logos and identity systems.
- Completed 30 projects and assisted with 12 others.
- Created and implemented print advertising campaign, which expanded client base 25% and brought in three new major customers.

Jan 1991-June 1991
Design Artist, Margaret Sloan Gallery, Titus University, PA
- Created a series of posters and postcards promoting professional and student work in the University galleries.
- Work was featured in a 1992 promotional brochure for the university.

EDUCATION

June 1991
Bachelor's Degree in Fine Arts, *Magna Cum Laude*, Titus University, PA
Minors: Computer Imaging, Drawing

AWARDS

1994
National Award Winner, American Paper Box Association
   Silver award in folding carton design
   Bronze award in ridged box design

1993
Finalist, National Print Magazine Cover Design Competition

1990
Accepted, Titus University Scholarship Show

1990
Scholarship Award for Outstanding Portfolio, National Card Co.

DOUGLAS R. HAUSMAN
77 E. Waverly
Durham, N.C. 27589
(919) 555-4598

SKILLS SUMMARY

Skilled communicator and manager with more than 10 years experience with state departments and agencies. Solid background in developing educational and informational programs. Adept at working with civic organizations, public officials and citizens in addressing complaints and requests for information.

PROFESSIONAL EXPERIENCE

June 1991-current

Director, Public Information Office
North Carolina State Health and Environment Department
Raleigh, N.C.

Direct all public information and public affairs activities of largest department in state. Manage community and media relations, publications and internal relations. Supervise staff of 15, including information specialists, graphic artists and clerical support.
* Increased placement of news and feature articles in newspapers, magazines and with radio and television stations by 34% in two years.
* Produce monthly newsletters, weekly fact sheets, brochures, public service announcements, videotape programs, displays and radio actualities, which report consistent, up-to-date information on department activities and findings.
* Recommended, developed and host talk show on local radio station, which enhances department's image and increases public awareness and feedback on critical issues.
* Designed program that pairs civic leaders with department officials, resulting in improved communication and understanding.

Oct 1989-June 1991

Information Specialist, Public Affairs Office
North Carolina State Highway Department
Durham, N.C.

Wrote and edited all news releases, public service announcements and biweekly newsletter. Wrote and produced radio actualities, public service announcements and video programs.
* Initiated educational program, which emphasized department's high success rate in completing projects on schedule and within budget.
* Worked with state fire and law enforcement agencies to establish Emergency Communication Plan for hazardous material spills.

(continued)

**PROFESSIONAL
EXPERIENCE**

Feb 1986-Oct 1989   **Public Information Officer and Citizen Assistance Section Manager**
Virginia Environmental Protection Agency
Richmond, Va.

Managed section that responds to complaints or requests for information from citizens and public officials. Maintained close relations with state and local civic organizations and special interest groups. Wrote news and feature articles.
* Initiated and conducted community educational programs, which provided information about agency activities and how they affect the public.
* Established and maintained large research library, which provided necessary materials for public use.
* Placed more than 250 articles statewide annually, increasing coverage 45%.
* Established new tracking and follow-up system for complaints and requests for information, which led to development of two new programs to address findings and meet citizens' needs.

June 1983-Feb 1986   **City Editor, Managing Editor**
Millville *News Journal*
Millville, Va.

Wrote news and feature stories, primarily on city government and politics. Promoted to managing editor March 1985. Assisted in directing paper's editorial policy and supervised work of other section editors.
* Earned five Virginia State Newspaper Association Awards, including special recognition for coverage of highly contested local political race, which centered on business and environmental issues.
* Initiated and wrote column highlighting current health-related and environmental issues, which helped educate the public and increase awareness.

EDUCATION

Duke University, Raleigh/Durham, N.C. (1990-1992)
* 12 graduate credit hours in organizational behavior (graduate level)

University of Virginia at Richmond (June 1983)
* Bachelor of Arts in Political Science/Journalism

ACTIVITIES

Director, Raleigh Metropolitan Park System Board

Susana T. Ramirez
50 El Paso Drive
Dallas, TX 75202
(214) 555-3029

SKILLS SUMMARY   Award-winning media relations expert with nearly 10 years of experience in virtually every aspect of public relations, including external media, customer newsletters, customer bill inserts, sponsorships, special events/promotions and contributions. Ability to manage a variety of media projects in creative ways. Excellent organizational, written and communication skills. Capable of successfully managing several projects simultaneously and meeting all deadlines.

EDUCATION   Master of Arts Degree in Public Relations *with honors*, University of Texas (1993)
Bachelor of Arts Degree *with honors*, Arizona State University (1987)

WORK EXPERIENCE

Public Relations Manager and Spokesperson, Teltech Communications, Dallas, TX   **1991-current**
Develop, recommend and manage communications strategies for informing the public of regional telecommunications company's many activities throughout the state. Promote company products, service, sponsorships and contributions. Serve as company spokesperson for media contacts about service outages.

- Edit residential customer newsletter and schedule printing to meet billing cycles.
- Generated more than $50,000 worth of media coverage statewide concerning Teltech's Texan Academic Super Bowl, with more than 150 articles in newspapers throughout the state.
- Initiated TelTech's sponsorship of Yuletide Celebration, a holiday presentation by the Dallas Symphony Orchestra; sponsorship has allowed symphony to bring in special guest artists and has enhanced company's image in the art and general communities.
- Developed and implemented hometown feature program where feature articles about employees in internal company publications are placed in hometown newspapers, increasing media coverage and enhancing public image.
- Wrote and placed five articles about company's technical research and development advancements in three trade magazines, recognizing and publicizing TelTech as a leader in the telecommunications industry.
- Assisted in developing and managing program through which community organizations received donations based on employee involvement; company contributes more than $25,000 annually to benefit its communities.

(continued)

124

WORK EXPERIENCE

Public Relations Administrator, Southwest Telephone, Phoenix, AZ   1989-1991
Wrote and distributed media relations materials for five-state regional telephone company.

- Served as bill insert and bill message coordinator for the entire region, including working with five state staffs to meet customer billing cycles.
- Handled media relations for company-sponsored golf tournament, including arranging press conferences, hosting and organizing the media tent and distributing daily press releases.
- Placed three technical articles in trade magazines, enhancing company's image as a technical leader.
- Organized sponsorship of Kids Day at the Zoo, where children from low-income households visited the zoo for free; enhanced company's image in the community.

Senior Writer, Public Relations, Arizona Department of Commerce, Phoenix, AZ   1987-1989
Administered communications functions in the areas of agriculture, economic development, energy and tourism. Wrote and distributed news releases about department activities.

- Wrote various agricultural and tourism speeches for Lieutenant Governor Watkins.
- Created a variety of publications, including handling photography, graphic design and printing.
- Recommended new tourism slogan, which appeared on promotional items from T-shirts to license plates and generated $2.5M in revenue.

AWARDS/
MEMBERSHIPS   Secretary, Assistant Treasurer, Dallas Chapter, International Association of Business Communicators
- Silver Quill Award of Excellence, Special Events Program
- Silver Quill Merit Award, Special Events Program
- Silver Quill Award of Excellence, External Newsletter

Scholarship Chair, Phoenix Chapter
Progress of Women in Communications Chair, Dallas Chapter
Women in Communications, Inc.
- Regional Competition Award of Excellence, Public Relations Campaign Series

Member, Texas Association of Event Professionals
- Honorable Mention Award, Best Promotional Item

Member, Public Relations Committee for Junior Achievement of Central Texas, Inc.

LISA J. BLEVINS

901 W. State Road 41
Willow, Neb. 68505

(402) 555-2331

SUMMARY OF SKILLS

- Ten years experience in professional news writing, feature writing and copy editing
- Ability to write accurately and effectively about a wide range of subject matter
- Skilled in interviewing, research and photography
- Adept in determining the "hook" that creates the strongest connection between the story and the audience

WORK HISTORY

July 1990-present **Writer/Editor, Independent School Management, Willow, Neb.**
- Edit all custom publications, including viewbooks and direct mail brochures, that reflect unique, individual programs of each school.
- Co-lead "Marketing Your School" and lead "Powerful Public Relations" workshops, which assist schools in presenting a specific image through admission materials, newsletters, advertising and working with the media.
- Create in-house marketing materials, such as catalogs, brochures and flyers, which have led to increased attendance at company workshops.
- Established and edit company's signature publication, which has repeatedly earned national recognition among independent school administrators and educators.

March 1993-present **Owner, Blevins Communications, Willow, Neb.**
- Created and edit Willow School District monthly newsletter and annual report, and handle all research, writing, graphics, design, typesetting and printing arrangements.
- Create brochures and flyers for local businesses and nonprofit organizations.

Jan 1985-July 1990 **Reporter/Managing Editor, The Frankfort Times, Frankfort, Neb.**
- Covered every type of story, from club activities and police reports to feature articles and major community news.
- Promoted to managing editor March 1988.
- Wrote editorials, columns and reviews, and edited correspondents' copy.
- Earned eight Nebraska journalism awards for writing.

EDUCATION

1985 Bachelor of Arts Degree in Journalism, University of Nebraska, Lincoln

ACTIVITIES

1992-present Volunteer, Lincoln Arts Alliance

SANDRA CHEN LU

95 W. Kimmel St.   (619) 555-2440 (home)
Glenview, CA 92332   (619) 555-2009 (work)

SUMMARY OF SKILLS

- Extensive legal experience in product liability, medical malpractice, contracts, real estate and personal injury litigation
- Trained and experienced in photography and in investigation and interviewing techniques
- Capable of working quickly and accurately under pressure to successfully meet short deadlines
- Able to analyze complex and detailed material and solve problems
- Effective oral and written communication skills
- Strong computer skills, including detailed knowledge of Wordperfect 5.1 and PageMaker

EDUCATION/CERTIFICATION

1990	NALA Certified Legal Assistant
1990	Certificate, California State University Paralegal Program
1991	Certificate, Litigation and Trial Practice, The Paralegal Institute
1992	Courses in Private Investigating and Photography, California State University Continuing Education Program
1993	Courses is Computer Software and Real Estate, Valley Vocational College, Springfield, CA

PROFESSIONAL EXPERIENCE

1990-current   **Litigation Paralegal, Warren, Pauley & Underhill, Glenview, CA**
- Interview clients, witnesses and experts to gather information for trial
- Prepare legal documents and settlement brochures
- Gather and interpret medical records and reports and provide written evaluation for attorneys
- Attend trials with litigation attorneys to provide information and assistance
- Research issues and cases and report findings to attorneys
- Investigated and discovered vital information for five $8M-$30M medical malpractice cases, two of which were well-publicized litigations; firm won all five cases
- Interviewed experts, reviewed documentation and completed legal research for three $15M- $50M product class action cases; firm won all three cases

PROFESSIONAL AFFILIATIONS

1993-current	Secretary, Treasurer, California Paralegal Association, Inc.
1991-current	President, Treasurer, Glen County Legal Personnel
1995-current	San Diego Bar Association

MARIANNE G. LISTER
45 E. Main St.
Waterloo, OR 97236
(503) 555-2093

Profile:

Extensive management experience and comprehensive banking background. Skilled in establishing new branch offices, policies and procedures. Experienced in developing investment and brokerage services.

Work Experience:
1993-current

Branch Manager, Society National Bank, Portland, OR
Supervise branch operations, new account personnel and investment department. Train all new employees.
- Guided branch through successful conversion to new computer system, products and procedures, resulting in enhanced customer service, more accessible records and better account report generation.
- Successfully established policy and procedures governing membership of the bank in the Portland Clearing House, Federal Reserve, Portland.

1990-1993

Assistant Manager, Society National Bank (formerly Home National Bank), Eugene, OR
Supervised daily branch operations, including teller line and new accounts. Managed vault operations. Trained new tellers.
- Managed buying/selling of currency for seven-branch network.
- Successfully established the bank's first branch office in the Portland market, creating new business opportunities for the bank, a new employer for the community and enhanced customer services.

1987-1990

Investment Officer, Home National Bank, Eugene, OR
Sold CDs, Treasury Bills/Bonds, U.S. Bonds, IRAs/QRPs and served as a discount broker.
- Established new IRA procedures and the bank's Discount Brokerage Service, expanding customer service offerings and creating new businesses for the bank.

1984-1987

Teller, Home National Bank, Eugene, OR
Handled teller duties, assisted in safe deposit box area and served as backup to loan, new account and investment departments.
- Successfully balanced branch's daily records.
- Recommended new procedure for businesses making large Monday morning deposits, enhancing service for those business customers and eliminating wait for personal account customers.

Education/Training:

National Banking Institute, Eugene, OR (1985-1987)
- Courses in investment banking, discount brokerage services and loan processing and monitoring
Graduate, Mantooth Memorial High School, Big Bend, OR (1984)

WENDY BARTHOLOMEW
15 Northside Dr.
Brighton, LA 71134
(318) 555-2556

**SUMMARY OF
QUALIFICATIONS**

- Experienced institutional food services manager with excellent background in menu planning, food preparation and dietary consultation
- Skilled in creating nutritious meals within a budget
- Experienced in supervising union employees, purchasing and forecasting

**PROFESSIONAL
EXPERIENCE**

1992-current

Food Service Director, MTE Corp., Martin Financial Services, Inc., Carthage, LA
- Supervise 20 employees providing service at corporate cafeteria
- Worked with corporate secretarial staff to develop catering specifications for employee banquets previously held off-site; corporation accepted bid, bringing in an additional $30,000 per year
- Created and introduced low-fat entree line, which increased sales $3,000 per month

1989-1992

Food Service Manager, MTE Corp., Brighton Community School Corp., Brighton, LA
- Supervised 30 employees at six school sites
- Handled personnel responsibilities, including hiring, dismissal, training and payroll
- Managed a $620,000 sales and $420,000 expense budget
- Interacted with people at all levels of the organization, including students, teachers, school board members and the administration
- Initiated new purchasing procedure on computer system, resulting in more accurate forecasting

1985-1989

Caterer, Marriott Educational Services, Southern University, Baton Rouge, LA
- Supervised and trained eight employees in food service
- Served as maitre d' at university president's home

1984-1985

Sales Clerk, Michael's Sportswear, Baton Rouge, LA
- Assisted customers in selecting clothing
- Helped design and arrange window displays
- Created "Mardi Gras" sales promotion, which increased sales 35% during promotion period

EDUCATION

1987

Bachelor of Science Degree in Supervision/Associate Degree in Applied Science in Restaurant, Hotel and Institutional Management, Southern University, Baton Rouge, LA (3.8/4.0)

GARY J. HENSLEY
51 S. Mayfield Dr.
Mobile, AL 36607
(205) 555-6003

SKILLS SUMMARY   Nearly 20 years management experience in the insurance industry. Solid background in premium auditing, product management, underwriting and computer systems management. Skilled in developing and implementing training programs, online policy systems and new products.

EMPLOYMENT HISTORY

January 1987-present   **National Insurance Company**
Mobile, AL
Premium Audit Manager (August 1994-present)
- Audit commercial book of business, including adjusting classifications and exposure.
- Communicate directly with independent agents to resolve audit disputes, which has enchanced working relationships between corporate office and field staff.
- Hire and train new staff on auditing guidelines and procedures.
- Supervise staff of five auditors and four support personnel.

Senior Staff Specialist, Product Management
(March 1993-August 1994)
- Integrated Underwriting System into Product Management Department, which involved evaluating and placing personnel in appropriate positions.
- Maintained "common" screens for Commercial Automated System.

Underwriting Systems Manager (November 1990-March 1993)
- Developed, implemented, trained and maintained corporate underwriting systems.
- Supervised staff of 30 with department budget in excess of $500,000.
- Provided training services to support automated and non-automated systems to 21 divisions and three service centers.
- Supervised maintenance of automated rate files for 40 states, supporting more than 2 million policies and $1.5 billion in written premiums.

Comline Systems Manager (January 1987-November 1990)
- Developed first commercial online policy issuing system for corporation.
- Implemented commercial online policy system in 15 divisions and three service centers.
- Developed training program and trained support personnel to maintain and enhance system.
- Supervised staff of 10.

(continued)

EMPLOYMENT HISTORY

June 1975-January 1987 **American Insurance Company**
Mobile, AL

Casualty Staff Specialist (April 1984-January 1987)
- Handled general liability, workers compensation and crime rates, rules and forms for all operating states.
- Created "Ultra Contractors," a commercial product that currently has more than $70 million of premium in force.
- Developed manuals to support rates, rules, forms and underwriting systems.
- Supervised staff of six.

Commercial Policy Service Manager, East Divisions (May 1981-April 1984)
- Managed all commercial rating, statistical coding and policy typing, representing more than $85 million premium dollars.
- Developed and implemented training program for commercial underwriting division.
- Supervised staff of 90.

Assistant Manager, Alabama Commercial Underwriting (July 1979-May 1981)
- Managed commercial underwriting and risk selection for approximately one-third of the state.
- Trained supporting underwriters, raters and typists.
- Supervised staff of 15.

Senior Commercial Underwriter (October 1977-July 1979)
- Handled risk selections and underwriting for lines of general liability, workers compensation, commercial auto, crime, plate glass and boiler and machinery.

EDUCATION

University of Alabama, Mobile
- 24 credit hours in General Studies (1974)

ACTIVITIES

Director, Mayfield Home Owners Association

Yee Su Wong
5216 Stone Ridge Rd.
Princeton, NJ 08544
(609) 555-3111

SKILLS SUMMARY   Nearly 15 years marketing experience with insurance and benefits. Skilled in creating innovative programs for corporate markets. Adept in developing products and programs across corporate lines. Solid background in developing products for benefits programs.

CAREER HISTORY

Vice President-Marketing, Hunter & Associates, Inc., Princeton, NJ   **May 1993-current**
Senior marketing officer for general insurance underwriter. Handle marketing and sales of all product lines, including stop loss health re-insurance, group life, flexible benefits and ancillary products. Manage all personnel and functions for six field offices.

- Managed premium growth to an annual rate of $64 million.

- Established new distribution system to increase flexible benefits software and administration sales, while realizing revenue from related individual product sales.

Manager-Corporate Sales, National Life Insurance Company, New York, NY   February 1989-May 1993
Managed sales in large corporation market, primarily through brokerage sources, by taking advantage of emerging market opportunities.

- Created innovative programs for corporate markets, such as integrating group and individual products, which helped expand client base.

- Expanded number of brokerage outlets and increased production from current brokers through relationship marketing, seminars and advertising.

(continued)

Manager-Marketing, National Life Insurance Company, New York, NY   **June 1987-February 1989**

Managed all marketing functions for 70 agencies and 1,500 agents, including advanced sales, training, payroll deduction plans, product promotion and incentives. Managed staff of 25 and $6 million budget.

- Designed and introduced new policy, which realized $15 million premium in its first two years.

- Introduced and edited agency newsletter, which provided sales/marketing information, helped close communication gap between home and field offices and provided consistency in information.

Manager-Marketing Operations, Pennsylvania Life, Philadelphia, PA   **May 1983-June 1987**

Managed all sales support areas, including advanced sales, management recruiting, training and conventions, for independent brokerage. Supervised staff of 15 and $1.5 million budget.

- Designed and launched six major new products in three years, generating 1986 premium revenue of more than $50 million.

Supervisor-Product Sales, Pennsylvania Life, Philadelphia, PA   **June 1982-May 1983**

Supervised advanced sales, product promotion and incentive program. Worked with 800 field agents. Handled all communication with field staff. Supervised office staff of three.

- Established incentive program for two new products, which generated premium revenue of more than $5 million.

- Initiated new marketing team, which designed short- and long-term goals for all life products.

EDUCATION   B.S., Business Administration, University of Kentucky, Louisville, with honors (1982)

MEMBERSHIPS   Association for Advanced Life Underwriting (AALU)
National Association of Life Underwriters (NALU)

Timothy L. Hinshaw
111 Wilshire Dr.
Memphis, TN 38127
(901) 555-0990

SKILLS SUMMARY   Excellent technical experience with strong background in mechanical engineering applications. Experienced in new facility set-up and management. Proven track record of exceeding all production, quality and cost goals. Trained and experienced in current quality engineering methods.

CAREER HISTORY

Manufacturing Manager, Hopewell Enterprises, Memphis, TN   **February 1993–current**
Start up and manage manufacturing and assembly facility for entrepreneurial company. Supervise production, engineering, human resources and maintenance. Design and implement optimum manufacturing processes for new products. Understand and comply with UL, FDA and NSF regulations.

- Designed, organized and set up new manufacturing facility below budget and ahead of schedule.
- Exceed all production, quality and cost goals in a fast-paced entrepreneurial environment.
- Serve as technical expert on all critical operations, which has resulted in improved production, assembly and quality processes.

Process Engineer, Worldwide Coatings, Knoxville, TN   **May 1990–February 1993**
Provided leadership and engineering solutions to technically complex problems and barriers. Designed and built new coating cells using the latest technology.

- Took charge of $500 million capital investment project to design/install three manufacturing cells in new plant.
- Recognized for developing new business growth.

Assistant Engineer, Worldwide Coatings, Knoxville, TN   **June 1989-May 1990**
Assisted in managing production, scheduling and training. Promoted in one year for rapidly handling assigned duties and aggressively seeking more responsibility.

- Developed and supervised processes for new product, which helped exceed projected production goals.

EDUCATION   B.S., Mechanical Engineering, with honors, University of Tennessee, Memphis (1989)

SUSAN FORD

1556 River Road
Talleyville, KS 66014
(913) 555-0332

SKILLS PROFILE

- Six years of office supervisory experience
- Skilled in developing successful office procedures
- Experienced in establishing collection plans and monitoring collection activity
- Accustomed to working in a fast-paced environment and successfully handling several responsibilities simultaneously

EMPLOYMENT HISTORY

Office Supervisor, William G. Morse, MD, Talleyville, KS (1992-current)
- Manage operation and maintenance of office equipment, maintain appropriate quantities of business supplies and maintain cost records and supply sources for all business supplies
- Established office payment plan program; arrange payment plans with patients; monitor those accounts to ensure compliance; prepare monthly report detailing collection activity; uncollected payments have fallen by 25%
- Perform administrative tasks such as distributing the mail, scheduling meetings and typing letters and documents
- Created and continue to update written job descriptions for office personnel
- Developed manual for all business office procedures, resulting in standardized operations
- Schedule daily appointments, handle phone communication, greet patients, collect payments and post accurate record of office charges and receipts into computer

Office Manager, Kevin D. McPherson, DDS, Knots, KS (1990-1992)
- Performed business office duties, such as payroll, accounts payable and accounts receivable, and balanced all accounts monthly
- Filed insurance claims and handled carrier requests
- Represented doctor's office in small claims court when filing against nonpaying clients
- Developed and maintained patient confirmation and no-show policies, which decreased no-shows by 50%

Receptionist, Kevin D. McPherson, DDS, Knots, KS (1989-1990)
- Scheduled daily appointments and handled phone communication
- Retrieved and filed charts for each day's patients; prepared new patient charts
- Collected and posted payments

Sales Clerk, Cramer Furniture, Talleyville, KS (1988-1989)
- Handled floor sales in lamps and dining room furniture
- Assisted with credit reporting, collections, bookkeeping and installment contracts
- Helped develop special sales and promotion plans, which led to 20% sales increase

EDUCATION

Warren County High School, Crown Point, KS (Graduated in June 1988)
Kansas Technical/Vocational College, Kansas City, KS (1988-1990)
        Related courses: accounting, computer operations, business communications

MIGUEL A. MARTINEZ
3330 Alden Way
Dallas, Texas 75255
(214) 555-2002

SKILLS PROFILE

- Manager with strong background in production control, machining center operations and tooling activities.
- Experienced in supervising manufacturing processes, from raw material to finished product.
- Skilled in using a variety of precision measuring instruments and in inspection procedures.
- Able to effectively communicate with individuals at all levels of an organization.

WORK EXPERIENCE
Oct 1987-current

Watkins, Inc., Dallas, Texas
Production Control Manager (May 1993-current)
Supervise planning, scheduling, production and shipment of products. Arrange work schedules to meet quantity and scheduling demands. Supervise more than 40 employees.

- Raised gross production levels 47% after 18 months, while significantly reducing man hours, errors and waste.
- Respond to daily changes in customer scheduling requirements, while maintaining 0 quality defects.
- Recommended and implemented new production training program, which reduced training time and improved employee performance.

Production Control Supervisor (Aug 1991-May 1993)
Assisted manager with all control phases of production process, including supervising all inspections. Worked directly with customers to determine and meet production schedules. Supervised 10 employees.

- Recommended new scheduling process, which helped company raise production levels 24%.
- Supervised installation and start-up of new plant equipment, ensuring a smooth transition and capability to meet scheduling demands.

CNC Machining Center Set-up Operator (Oct 1987-Aug 1991)
Wrote machine programs, set up and operated LeBlond-Makino and Kitamura Mycenter machining centers.

- Determined points of intersection and all necessary data to manufacture quality productions to tolerances as close as $\pm.0005$.
- Earned Employee of the Year Award for suggestion that reorganized center to enhance work flow and increase production.

(continued)

WORK EXPERIENCE

Jan 1983-Oct 1987

Texas Locks, Dallas, Texas
Tooling Coordinator
Coordinated all tooling activities and provided support to production line.
Supervised two employees.
* Redesigned tool crib, which improved work flow through better organized work stations.
* Established bin balance system.

Feb 1982-Jan 1983

Precision Products, Dallas, Texas
Set-Up Operator
Worked with multi-spindle, automatic screw machines.
* Coordinated service and warranty work with equipment companies.
* Designed new maintenance program, which reduced down-time 33% and enhanced ability to meet customer schedules.

June 1980-Feb 1982

Spitz & Co., Dallas, Texas
Service Representative
Installed new Mackey Automatic Multiple Spindle Screw Machines and performed on-site warranty and service at 25 Southwest plants.
* Earned company's Outstanding Customer Service Award for 1981.

EDUCATION

Riviera Community College, Riviera, Texas (1990-1993)
* 12 credit hours in management

Woodland Vocational College, Woodland, Texas (1983-1986)
* Nine credit hours in computer science
* Six credit hours in computer programming
* Six credit hours in trigonometry and pre-calculus

ACTIVITIES

Eagle Scout Leader, Troup #51, Dallas, Texas

Cynthia J. Snyder • 215 Kelley Rd. • Honolulu, HI • 96845 • (808) 555-9804

Summary of Qualifications

Engineer and manager with seven years production and operations experience. Skilled in team building and in implementing employee involvement and quality control programs to increase morale and performance. Proven track record of exceeding production, quality, safety and financial goals.

Professional Experience

Operations Manager, TileTex, Inc., Honolulu, HI
(November 1993-present)

Manage and control manufacturing facility. Handle processes, procedures, human resources and financial performance. Work with limited administrative support, which requires ability to "wear all hats." Serve as liaison with headquarters' corporate staff and sales team in Chicago.

- Recommended use for manufacturing by-product that has generated nearly $2 million annually in sales.
- Established fully computerized operations with Chicago office, saving $20,000 annually in telephone and facsimile expenses.
- Initiated one-on-one review process with top customers to ensure customer satisfaction and meet or exceed quality standards; have retained 100% of the customers.

Production Supervisor, Suprex Industries, Honolulu, HI
(August 1988-November 1993)

Supervised production, scheduling and training activities and assisted production manager in cooperation/support of joint venture customers. Provided technical leadership.

- Initiated use of Total Quality Control and Employee Involvement programs to achieve highest output in 12 years (65% increase over previous year).
- Managed start up of new facility, implemented team concept and achieved performance standards that exceeded first-year goal by 20%.
- Commended by division president for creating/leading teams, supervising successful new plant start up and exceeding production, quality and safety standards.

Education

Bachelor of Science in Mechanical Engineering, *Magna Cum Laude*, Case Western Reserve University, Cleveland, OH (1988)

EDWARD CHANG
23 West Alamedo Blvd
San Diego, CA 92203
(619) 555-3400

SKILLS PROFILE

Manager with 10 years experience in production, supervision and quality control. Skilled in counseling customers on quality issues, establishing quality standards and solving quality-related problems. Capable of managing product conformance from raw material to final inspection.

WORK EXPERIENCE

May 1991-current

Quality Manager, Midway Engineering, San Diego, CA
Supervise three inspectors in manufacturing of sheet metal and machine tools for major aircraft and automotive firms.
- Manage internal quality of manufacturing records, certifications and requirements of individual customers.
- Handle internal and supplier audits and implementation of SPC.
- Raised quality rating with major customer from 60% to 100% in two years; no rejections in three years; resulted in Certified Supplier status and no-inspection status for goods shipped to customer from production plant.
- Recommended and implemented new process, which increased production by 25% without jeopardizing quality.

June 1988-May 1991

Inspection Supervisor, Tube Forming, Corp., Marshall, CA
Inspected in-process, welding, flouropenetrant and final assembly.
- Handled fabrication, layout of aircraft engine tubing and components for major aircraft companies.
- Implemented new inspection process, which identified and led to correction of potential defects.
- Helped implement mock-up thrust reverse assembly for W360 aircraft.

Jan 1986-June 1988

Production Supervisor, Transmission Suppliers, Inc., Marshall, CA
- Supervised manufacturing and grinding of friction wafers for bonding to clutch and transmission parts, meeting tolerances of ±001.
- Recommended new process, resulting in fewer casting cracks, higher product quality and $3 million in new business.
- Established new production procedure, which increased units produced by 35%.
- Wrote new quality manual, which established product specifications and standards necessary to meet customer requirements.

EDUCATION
1986

B.S. in Business Management, *With Distinction*, San Diego State University

ROSA B. ORTIZ
422 W. Ridge Rd.
Kansas City, KS 66136
(913) 555-0090

SKILLS SUMMARY

Manager and corporate trainer with solid background in developing training programs and computer software materials. Skilled in providing hands-on field service and ensuring client satisfaction. Extensive insurance and marketing experience.

WORK HISTORY
1994-current

Training and Field Service Manager
AllNet Financial Corp.
Kansas City, KS

Train medical and dental providers on patient finance program and practice management software. Serve as liaison between providers, sales staff and administrative staff.

- Developed all corporate training and marketing materials for medical financing program and practice management software.
- Designed and assisted with software programming, which supports current products.
- Evaluate client needs and conform policies and procedures to best suit client needs, while staying within legal and operational constraints.
- Communicate with clients to ensure satisfaction with program and provide education to resolve potential conflicts.

1991-1994

Corporate Trainer
West Bend Mutual Insurance Company
Lawrence, KS

Provided training for headquarters executives and professionals in 50 branch offices throughout the country.

- Developed and maintained a series of training manuals and tests, which were used to evaluate the continued employment of the student.
- Conducted several classroom-style training sessions for specific technical functions.
- Created self-study program, which increased productivity by allowing student to study outside of classroom.

(continued)

WORK HISTORY

1989-1991

Client Service Supervisor
West Bend Mutual Insurance Company
Lawrence, KS

Supervised department of 18 service representatives that received all incoming client inquiries.
- Reduced client response time from 60 days to one day in just two months.
- Established first-ever comprehensive training program, which resulted in a more productive and efficient staff.

1987-1989

Marketing Promotions Manager
Walters Marketing, Inc.
Kansas City, MO

Generated sales leads for major recreational manufacturer. Located and negotiated exhibit areas in trade shows, malls and fairs in tri-state area.
- Selected to travel to other branch locations to hire, train and motivate new managers.
- Consistently increased leads by 46% through effective management techniques.
- Earned Manager of the Year award (1988).

EDUCATION

University of Kansas, Lawrence
- 18 hours of graduate studies in management and training (1991-1993)
- Bachelor of Science in Marketing (1987)

ACTIVITIES

Publicity Committee, Kansas City Arts Alliance
Big Sister, Tri-County Big Sisters, Inc.

Randall R. Gibbs
935 Pheasant Run
Cheyenne, WY 82002
(307) 555-2993

Skills Summary

Skilled manager with creative, innovative approach to managing staff, generating teamwork and improving customer service. Proven track record of low turnover, low overtime, high retention rate and high profit.

Employment

Assistant Manager/Service Manager, The Steak House, Cheyenne, WY (November 1994-current)

Manage, train and schedule up to 90 employees for 250-seat restaurant, including wait staff, hostesses, bus boys and bar staff. Manage all aspects of customer service. Promoted from assistant manager to service manager in one month.
- Created monthly employee newsletter, which presents franchise policies and procedures in nonconfrontational manner and improves knowledge of restaurant business; regional manager has recognized and adopted publication for regional use.
- Developed customer hand-out card, which explains seating procedures for large parties and provides suggested activities for guests while they wait to be seated.
- Initiated "roaming manager" approach to receive customer feedback and address problems or concerns; customer satisfaction rate currently highest in region.
- Revised and color-coded seating chart, which helps new employees learn stations and alerts kitchen staff when stations close.
- Maintain lowest overtime and turnover in region; retention rate 44% above company standard, saving $23,000 annually.
- Exceeded 1994's gross margin profits by 24%.

Kitchen Manager, The Steak House, Casper, WY (June 1993-November 1994)

Supervised up to 20 cooks and dish area employees for 150-seat restaurant.
- Redistributed clean-up assignments to even out duties, which improved employee teamwork and morale.
- Initiated safety program, which reduced on-the-job injuries 40%; program adopted and implemented throughout region.

Head Waiter, Alpha Xi Delta Sorority, University of Wyoming, Laramie (School years 1991-1993)

Supervised wait staff of seven and assigned serving and clean-up duties.
- Initiated recognition program, which honored wait staff for attendance and work quality; reduced high turnover/no-show rate.

Waiter/Assistant Manager, Quail Inn, Laramie, WY (Summers 1991-1993)

Provided customer service. Filled in as assistant manager when necessary.
- Developed and implemented customer satisfaction survey, which helped improve service and increased patronage.

Education

Manager Training Program, The Steak House, Cheyenne, WY (June-August 1993)
B.S. in Restaurant/Hotel Management, University of Wyoming, Laramie (1991)

Elaine Godfrey • 901 E. Vine St. • Huntington, MO • 65326 • (816) 555-5423

Summary of Qualifications

Eleven years providing office administrative and clerical support, including handling confidential information. Skilled in word processing and accounting software, including Lotus 1-2-3 and WordPerfect. Accustomed to meeting tight deadlines. Excellent telephone, filing, interpersonal and organizational skills. Experienced in meeting planning and travel arrangements.

Work Experience

Administrative Assistant, PowerPlay, Inc., St. Louis, MO
October 1990 - present
* Schedule monthly meetings and handle travel arrangements for 17 field and regional headquarters staff members; prepare all necessary paperwork and audio/visual materials; make meal and hotel arrangements; process travel expense reports
* Prepare all written correspondence, invoices and administrative reports for department manager
* Track budget and prepare quarterly reports
* Implemented Electronic Mail system for field staff, resulting in faster communication and quicker responses to headquarters' requests
* Trained clerical staff in accounting computer software, saving outside training expenses of $2,000

Senior Clerk, Power Play, Inc., St. Louis, MO
May 1988 - October 1990
* Provided clerical support for secretarial and associate staff
* Prepared all department's computerized graphs, charts and visual presentation aids
* Standardized department filing system so secretarial staff could easily locate information in any filing center

Records Clerk, Huntington Home Bank, Huntington, MO
February 1986 - May 1988
* Recorded and filed employee benefit, salary and annual evaluation information
* Assisted with payroll preparation and entered data on keypunch machine
* Served as liaison between computer room and payroll supervisor and managed delivery and pick-up of confidential information
* Sponsored department's participation in community walk-a-thon fund drive; department won highest participation award and third-highest per-capita donation award

Volunteer Experience

Church Secretary, Huntington United Methodist Church, Huntington, MO
January 1985 - January 1986
* Prepared all written communication, answered telephones and prepared weekly bulletins
* Designed and implemented Master Schedule and User Guidelines for church and community meetings and weddings, which reduced scheduling conflicts and building maintenance costs

Education

Owen Tech Vocational School, Salisbury, MO (January 1985 - January 1986)
* Computer Operations
* Business Communication
* Office Management

Carol A. Lafferty • 1442 W. Wilshire Ct. • Oklahoma City, OK • 73102 • (405) 555-9822

Summary of Qualifications

Skilled administrator with nearly 10 years experience in executive administration, marketing and sales management, including program and trade show coordination. Solid background in office computer operations, office administration and training.

Professional Experience

Wellington Commercial Air Filters, Oklahoma City, OK
Executive Administrator, North American Products Group (August 1994-current)
Provide administrative and advisory support for corporate president and all international/regional vice presidents.
* Coordinate and implement international corporate projects, policies, procedures, ventures and acquisitions.
* Implemented standardized office computer operations and software for domestic operations, with international implementation set for June 1997.

Executive Assistant, Automotive & Consumer Group (April 1992-August 1994)
Handled administrative and advisory support for corporate president. Coordinated progress reporting and assignments of vice presidents. Planned and coordinated arrangements for all corporate meetings.
* Developed orientation and training program for administrative secretaries, which increased efficiency and productivity and reduced overlapping duties.
* Managed marketing and promotion of automotive racing program, which produced high name recognition for corporation domestically and abroad.

Marketing Assistant, Automotive & Consumer Group (November 1989-April 1992)
Served as corporate assistant to consumer and automotive marketing vice presidents, national sales managers and senior product managers. Provided marketing support to 200-member sales force. Assisted in promoting automotive racing program.
* Compiled and analyzed sales/marketing reports, oversaw new product implementation and supervised customer inquiries.
* Implemented new competitive analysis procedure, which helped establish short- and long-term corporate marketing goals.

Marketing Professionals International, Tulsa, OK
Program Administrator-Affiliate Services (July 1986-November 1989)
Provided administrative support management for 15,000-member trade organization. Supervised all programs undertaken by 100 affiliated organizations. Handled public speaking, membership development, convention and program planning, trade show coordination, and printing and advertising for all marketing promotions.
* Increased membership 25% in two years.

Education

Bachelor of Science in Business Administration, Tulsa State College, Tulsa, OK (1986)
* Concentration in Administrative Management

Justin A. Shaffer
56 N. Alamogordo Dr.
Phoenix, AZ 85002
(602) 555-4667

Profile

Skilled manager with five years experience in directing employee recruitment, training and evaluation activities. Solid background in developing and implementing progressive and innovative evaluation and training programs to improve employee morale and reduce turnover.

Experience

Human Resources Manager, Tuttle Enterprises, Phoenix, AZ (May 1993–current)

Manage employee recruiting, evaluation and training programs and procedures for company with 1,500 employees. Review internal and external candidate applications and coordinate interviews with appropriate department and section heads.

- Established new performance evaluation and tracking procedure, which has increased employee satisfaction with review process 45%.
- Recommended and implemented automated, self-paced training program that provides employees with opportunity to acquire needed skills for advancement on company computers and company time.
- Reduced employee turnover 25% by June 1994.

Military Personnel Management/Programs Officer, Arizona Air National Guard, Midway Field, AZ (February 1990-May 1993)

Directed military personnel programs for Arizona Air National Guard (approximately 3,300 members). Established, implemented and managed personnel policies, incentive and promotion programs and personnel utilization.

- Managed office automation systems and trained all personnel on computer use, software and hardware.
- Increased office support capabilities and decreased required overtime by 50%.
- Became central coordinator for headquarters' enlisted members, including work assignments, training, awards, decoration and promotion; innovative efforts led to documented positive impact on enlisted members' performance, production and morale.

Education

B.S. in Business Administration, Arizona State University, Phoenix (1991)

Arizona Commendation Medal as Honor Graduate, Personnel Programs Officer Training, United States Air Force, Phoenix, AZ (December 1992)

Theresa Knapp
401 Hunter's Way
Hewes, CA 92182
(619) 555-2003

SKILLS SUMMARY

Award-winning account executive with strong background in computer system sales, multi-national territory management, end-user prospecting, competitive engagements, complex contract negotiations and third-party software partnerships. Excellent experience in financial analysis and in forecasting sales revenue, volume, discounting and profit. Proven ability to consistently exceed sales goals.

PC application skills: Windows 3.1, Word, Excel, PowerPoint

WORK EXPERIENCE

Major Account Executive, Advanced Computer Systems, Reading, CA   **1994-current**
Develop new territory in district, including several Fortune 500 accounts, such as Levi Strauss and Esprit.

- Market and sell large-scale, UNIX and Windows NT symmetric multiprocessing servers and professional services as solutions for companies moving from proprietary to open systems.
- Generate prospects for applications, including manufacturing, financials, decision support, enterprise messaging and enterprise architecture planning.
- Prospect for new business through various marketing campaigns, including telemarketing, direct mail, targeted seminars and partnerships with leading software firms.
- Recommended new territory management approach, which netted 15 new clients and a 45% sales increase.

Marketing & Finance Staff, PFE Corp., Los Angeles, CA   **1992-1994**
Promoted to staff assignment to broaden experience and prepare for sales management.

- Handled financial analysis and planning for $4 billion Western U.S. sales and services.
- Forecasted sales revenue, volumes, discounting and profit for company vice president.
- Assigned sales quota to 20 regional managers covering 10 states.
- Earned two Finance Director's awards for forecasting and sales quota management.

(continued)

WORK EXPERIENCE

International Account Manager, PFE Corp., Los Angeles, CA   **1988-1992**

Managed worldwide $10 million sales quota for Fortune 500 account, including complete line of products and services. Handled sales volume of more than $25 million.

- Directed $500,000 3-D apparel CAD application to reduce time-to-market delays and enhance retail sales operations.
- Ranked in top three of PFE's 30 sales representatives.
- Posted 110% to 135% quota performance with four consecutive 100% Clubs.
- Earned Regional Manager's award for first new $5 million mainframe at Fortune 500 company.
- Won competitive bids over other major computer product and service providers, including AT&T and IBM.

Manufacturing Management, PFE Corp., Los Angeles, CA   **1983-1988**

Supervised technical activities and 30 employees at company production plant.

- Designed manufacturing facilities, planned capital budgets and presented investment business cases to plant manager.
- Consistently exceeded production schedules while achieving 99.5% defect-free quality.
- Evaluated and recommended new process which helped plant exceed production objectives while 15% understaffed.
- Earned Outstanding Manager's award for leading department's turnaround success.

EDUCATION   B.S., Industrial Engineering, *Cum Laude*, California Polytechnical Institute

ACTIVITIES   Fundraising Chairman, Kappa Kappa Kappa philanthrophic organization, Omega
            Chapter
            Advisor, Junior Achievement Club of Hewes, CA

Michael Swinger
5623 North State Road 46
Advance, IA 52203
(319) 555-2034

Skills Summary

Top salesman with extensive background in agricultural sales. Specialized technical knowledge in animal nutrition and herd management. Experienced in developing computerized record-keeping systems. Excellent analytical skills–a student of current and developing market trends. Also skilled in developing new agricultural accounts for 50,000-watt radio station. Additional experience in supervision and production management.

Employment

Area Sales Representative, Macon Feeds, Inc., Des Moines, IA (1992-present)
- Handle feed sales for four-county territory, generating $400,000 annually in sales.
- Recognized as one of company's top 10 salespeople each year since 1992.
- Increased number of customers by 20% in two years.
- Helped create and implement F.O.B. feed delivery system, which allowed customers to call 800 number to place an order, enhancing customer service and increasing territory sales by 25%.
- Implemented computerized swine record-keeping program, resulting in better report generation and improved feed analysis and herd management.

Agricultural Account Representative, AAAA Radio, Linden, IA (1988-1992)
- Handled 40 agricultural accounts in the 40-mile radius listening area (50,000 watts).
- Developed 10 new accounts in first year with the station.
- Improved national account status by 30%.
- Managed $250,000 sales budget.
- Organized weekend radio auctions and supervised staff of three who obtained price-reduced or donated items/services from local businesses, resulting in profitable air time for the station and positive advertising results for the businesses.

Sales Representative, Holmstead Mills, Inc., Davenport, IA (1984-1988)
- Handled feed sales for two counties, generating $250,000 in annual sales.
- Counseled customers on feed products and nutrition management.
- Assisted customers in assessing feed needs and developing goals.
- Achieved top salesperson status (first in 1988), earning four incentive trips.
- Served on team to develop company's computerized record-keeping system, resulting in more accurate customer records and improved product sales and account analysis.

(continued)

Shift Supervisor, Third Shift Superintendent, American Chain Co., Des Moines, IA (1982-1984)
- Supervised up to 200 union employees in manufacturing facility.
- Managed production, disciplinary action, budget, material handling, safety and quality control.
- Promoted after one year to superintendent.
- Implemented and assisted industrial engineering department in layout and moving of heavy chain assembly to another area of the plant, resulting in a smooth transition and only four hours of production down time (budgeted time was 12 hours).
- Revised and implemented new procedure in assembly department, resulting in productivity increase of 25%.

Supervisor, National Filters, Warren, IA (1979-1982)
- Supervised up to 30 union employees in a production plant.
- Worked with human resources department to design a new safety program, reducing on-the-job injuries by 30%.
- Recommended new product and distribution system, which opened up business opportunities in three new market areas.

Education

Graduate Studies in Economics and Marketing, Iowa State University (1992-1993)

Bachelor of Science Degree in Business Management, University of Iowa (1979)

Related Affiliations

Director, White County Pork Producers, White County, IA (1992-current)

Officer, Consignment Sale Chairman, White County Young Farmers, White County, IA (1993-current)
- Established and organize annual consignment sale with high school vocational agricultural department.
- Raise nearly $3,000 annually.

Tammy Oberforce

45 Tacoma Dr.
East Bend, NM 87033
(505) 555-2003

SKILLS PROFILE

- Ten years experience in retail sales, including purchasing, inventory management and advertising.
- Skilled in developing successful sales promotions.
- Experienced in training and managing sales staffs.
- Skilled in customer account management.
- Strong computer skills.

EMPLOYMENT HISTORY

Department Manager, McKesson Hardware and Gifts, Mesa, AZ (1992-present)
- Manage purchasing and inventory for housewares department, which generates annual sales of $250,000.
- Introduced and handled sales promotions for new housewares product line, resulting in increased sales of 30%.
- Initiated new advertising strategies, which enhanced customer image of store and increased customer traffic.
- Worked with other local retailers to establish "Summer Sizzle Sidewalk Day," including retailer discounts, craft booths and fund-rasing activities for local civic organizations.
- Design and arrange window display for housewares section.
- Manage staff of three and train all new sales employees.

Sales Clerk/Bookkeeper, McKesson Hardware and Gifts, Mesa, AZ (1989-1992)
- Handled floor sales for housewares and gift departments.
- Organized special holiday sales promotion and recommended special holiday gift line, which increased sales by 35%.
- Established new accounts, posted accounts receivable and prepared and sent monthly statements.
- Reviewed past-due accounts with clients and established payment plans.
- Recommended computerized bookkeeping and supervised all data entry, resulting in reduced bookkeeping time, detailed department reports, improved sales projections, and enhanced business, advertising and budget planning.

Sales Clerk, Sears & Roebuck Co., Mesa, AZ (Summers 1985-1989)
- Handled floor and cash register sales in hardware, paint and housewares departments.
- Assisted in training new sales clerks.
- Suggested new display idea for housewares product, which improved customers' view of–and accessibility to–the product, resulting in increased sales.

EDUCATION

Graduate, Mesa Community High School, Mesa, AZ (1989)

Margaret Schuette
1021 Miller Ct.
Columbus, OH 43298
(614) 555-6304

SKILLS PROFILE

- Solid background in business analysis and long-range strategic planning.
- Skilled in leading teams of diverse backgrounds to make sound business decisions based on analyses of short- and long-term business needs.
- Able to take a large conceptual problem or project, break it into components, establish plans and a critical path, achieve incremental goals and deliver project on time and at or below budget.

PROFESSIONAL
EXPERIENCE

North America AgChem, Columbus, OH
Sr. Business Analyst (1994-current)
Work cross-functionally with marketing, manufacturing, research and development, legal and finance to balance product lines and determine business strategy.

- Established new financial analysis procedure for marketing plans, which has redirected more than $5 million in unprofitable marketing expenditures to more productive areas, such as product development.
- Restructured portfolio for research group, which provides guidelines for determining company funding for current and future projects and aids in long-range budgeting and business planning.
- Serve as controller for $162 million agricultural chemical product group.

Sr. Contract Manufacturing Administrator (1991-1994)
Led teams of various disciplines, such as sales, scientists and manufacturing staffs, in problem-solving, cost planning and quality control of various products.

- Successfully managed formulation of $31.5 million agricultural products at third-party manufacturing sites across the country.
- Developed long-range strategy for agricultural chemical product, which fully utilized in-house capacity and limited company exposure to cross-contamination potential at third-party sites.

Business Specialist-Site Operations (1989-1991)
Completed in six months and on schedule a project that established all services for new, 1.3 million-square-foot complex on 325 acres, ensuring smooth transition to new facilities.

- Supervised more than 80 people in delivering all services to three companies at new site.
- Developed procedures for working with managed services with an annual budget of $2.5 million.
- Worked with contractors to set performance standards, monitor performance, suggest improvements and ensure compliance.

EDUCATION

M.B.A., The Ohio State University (1993)
B.S. in Business Management, Bowling Green University, OH (1989)

Christina H. Chin • 809 W. Freeman St. • Columbia, S.C. • 29230 • (803) 555-6777

Summary of Qualifications

Nearly eight years experience in the insurance field, with emphasis on quality review. Skilled in creating, implementing and conducting internal and external audit programs, including analyzing statistical reports, accounting reviews and conducting staff interviews. Solid training and communication skills.

Experience

Eastern Warren, Inc., Columbia, S.C. (August 1990-current)
(A subsidiary of Eastern Insurance Group)

Director of Quality Review (Auditing), (November 1992-current)
Manage department and five professional-level employees. Audit external clients and internal staff to ensure maximum operational efficiency. Develop business plan and department budget. Handle staff training, administration and motivation.
- Create, test and implement all audit programs.
- Continually evaluate effectiveness of audit programs and report statistics to Executive Committee.
- Identified three problem areas for major client and designed specialized audit to monitor progress, which has resulted in improved operations and work flow.

Quality Review Auditor (August 1990-November 1992)
Conducted and reported on various types of internal and external audits, encompassing a variety of operational functions in the insurance field.
- Conducted on-site aggregate claim audits to determine proper reimbursement to clients by reviewing claims, premium, eligibility and contract interpretation.
- Conducted on-site operational audits; used statistical reports, claim, premium, accounting and eligibility reviews, and one-on-one interviews with client's staff.
- Conducted on-site approval audits, which allowed management committee to evaluate client's abilities and professional competency; used staff interviews, systems reviews and monitored administrative techniques.

Smithton Life Insurance Company of South Carolina, Columbia, S.C.
(A subsidiary of Eastern Insurance Group)

Claims Supervisor (June 1988-August 1990)
Managed department and seven claim examiners and support staff. Administered group and individual life, disability income and medical benefits. Developed business plan and department budget. Handled staff training and administration.
- Assisted and advised staff in making claim decisions and continually evaluated accuracy of decisions.
- Reviewed and translated insurance contracts.
- Organized and supervised daily work flows to ensure maximum productivity.
- Reduced claims response time from 30 days to two days after just six months on the job.

Education

General Studies, University of Florida, Miami, Fla. (1986-1988)
- 12 credit hours in business administration

KENNETH G. LAMBERT
2015 Park St.
Bozeman, MT 59715
(406) 555-0224

OBJECTIVE

To secure capital and investors for business expansion.

PROFILE

Award-winning business owner with more than seven years experience in management, marketing, sales and training. Skilled in determining, developing and securing funding for successful business growth.

EXPERIENCE
May 1990-current

Owner, Gadgets, Gifts & Gear, Bozeman, MT
Own and manage business, which provides variety of hardware, gifts and clothing. Handle all aspects of business, including customer service, sales, purchasing, accounting and employee hiring and training.
- Expanded hardware line in 1992 to include small appliances and gifts, which nearly doubled sales in one year.
- Grew business from two employees and annual sales of $300K to 12 employees and annual sales of $1.5M in three years.
- Tapped into tourist trade in 1994 by offering quality, name-brand outdoor clothing and fishing supplies, which increased sales 20%.

August 1988-March 1990

Manager, Clem's Camping Supplies, Bozeman, MT
Supervised all floor sales and trained sales staff. Managed inventory, purchasing and customer service.
- Assisted owner in enhancing store's physical appearance, which increased customer traffic.
- Introduced new line of protective gear, which increased sales 35% in one year.

July 1986-August 1988

River Guide, Fly Fishing Tours, Inc., Bozeman, MT
Led group fly fishing tours, including five-day, overnight camping trips.
- Earned Top Guide Award 1987-1988.

PROFESSIONAL
ORGANIZATIONS

Vice President, Northwest America Hardware Association
- Help determine services for all hardware stores in five-state area.
- Named Outstanding Store Manager-Growth (1993).

Board Member, Young Hardware Professionals
- Currently working on networking program to assist young hardware professionals.

ACTIVITIES

Parade Committee Chairman, Bozeman Fall Festival
Fly fishing

EDUCATION

Business Courses, University of Montana, Helena (1984-1986)

Brian Holloway
336 N. Salem Ave.
Cincinnati, OH 45205
(513) 555-8282

SKILLS SUMMARY   Extensive background in grain merchandising and commodity exporting on inland waterways and truck lines. Skilled in expanding business by developing new customers and services. Adept at contract negotiation and managing risk aspects for commodities. Experienced in export bagging operations and direct transfer business.

CAREER HISTORY

Director, Haverford Barge Company, Cincinnati, OH   **October 1992-current**
Responsible for profit/loss for $1.5M export facility. Provide general terminal services sales for 12 Midwest river facilities.

- Manage daily merchandising and personnel for Ohio export facility, which has achieved gross sales of more than $40M in last two years, a 45% increase.
- Oversee labor supply and services contract from third party.
- Negotiate all purchases and sales contracts with exporters.
- Expanded business by developing new European customers in Spain, France and Portugal.
- Quantify and manage all risk aspects for commodities and negotiate all freight and FOB arrangements.
- Represent and sell transfer services to various large customers that use one or more transfer points.
- Package rail, barge and transfer rates for river loading/unloading stations.

Sales/ Special Projects Manager, Haverford Barge Company, Cincinnati, OH   **May 1989-October 1992**
Coordinated all sales work for products other than whole grain at largest river facility.

- Handled all customer contracts and sales for 750,000-ton fertilizer warehouse, export bagging operation and more than 500,000 tons of direct transfer business received on an annual basis.
- Completed contracts with ocean freight companies for bagging contracts and took program to more than 40,000 short tons in the first year.
- Developed and directed small fleet of owners/operators to expand business and take advantage of various seasonal trucking opportunities.
- Negotiated and implemented a contract with a major firm to stevedore all capital equipment installed in a new auto manufacturing plant at Evansville, Ind.

(continued)

CAREER HISTORY

Grain Merchandiser/Special Projects Manager, Inland Transport, St. Louis, MO	**June 1987-May 1989**

Director, Inland Truck Line, St. Louis, MO
One of two merchandisers responsible for originating grain on an FOB truck basis in four Plains states. Became director of Inland Truck Line in 1988.

- Completed daily balancing of all position and hedging activity.
- Supervised five employees on second-shift barge loading crew.
- Expanded services by establishing truck line and acquiring necessary regulatory approval to transport various commodities, including steel, scrap, ore and coal.
- Grew operation from one to three full-time employees.
- Exceeded all first-year forecasts by netting $170,000.

Grain Merchandiser, Inland Transport, St. Louis, MO	**June 1984-June 1987**

One of three merchandisers responsible for originating grain from farmers and elevators in three Midwest states.

- Maintained daily position balancing reports, month-end accounting and projections.
- Recommended and implemented procedures for delayed pricing positions and spread positions, which were incorporated at all company facilities.
- Helped establish and assisted in daily operation of new subsidiary, which transported general commodities throughout the 48 contiguous United States.

EDUCATION B.S., Agricultural Economics, University of Illinois, Champaign/Urbana (1984)

Sara Gutierrez • 23 Marsh Road • Woodbridge, New York • 10912 • (914) 555-2009

Summary of Qualifications

Eight years of experience in programming, system development and system administration. Extensive UNIX background. Comprehensive knowledge of personal computer software, hardware and peripherals. Well-versed in delivering technical presentations. Outstanding analytical skills. Seasoned Internet user.

Programming Languages

C/C++, Pascal, Empress 4GL, SQL, Embedded SQL, FORTRAN, Perl, BASIC

Platforms

IRIS workstation, MS DOS, MS Windows, Interactive 386 UNIX, Macintosh, VAX

Work Experience

Programmer/Analyst, New World Systems, Whitehall, NY

(July 1993-current)

- Enhance and support a relational database application used by the U.S. Government.
- Handle software development, database administration, system administration, future requirements planning, PC hardware/software support, user support and daily operations.
- Implemented major improvements in automation of administrative and operational procedures, including distributed-database updates and data integrity checks, data transmission processes, managerial status reports and data backup, which allows programmers more time to work on upgrade and development tasks.
- Reduced client's operating and maintenance costs by porting code from mainframe to code on microcomputer systems.
- Worked with Interactive UNIX and a variety of other languages and platforms to complete project.

Programmer/Designer, Lincoln Research Center, Sun City, FL

(May 1988-July 1993)

- Investigated new fuselage design techniques for advanced aircraft design using computational fluid dynamics and unstructured-mesh computer modeling of aircraft geometries.
- Conducted a space vehicle packaging study using specialized CAD software and computational hypersonic aerodynamic models.
- Worked as part of a research team studying turboprop configurations in a low-speed wind tunnel, which led to improved aircraft design and performance.
- Upgraded and corrected a sonic-boom prediction program, which provided more accurate measurements and information.

Education

B.S. in Aeronautics, Massachusetts Institute of Technology, May 1988, *Cum Laude*

Other occupations

education, engineering, government, nonprofit, environmental, social service, health care, mental health, skilled trades

Abigail Scott
45 Stone Court
Williamsburg, PA 17704
(717) 555-4554

CAREER OBJECTIVE

To secure a full-time teaching position at the kindergarten to third-grade level.

SKILLS PROFILE

- Develop and implement lesson plans for all areas of a developmentally appropriate curriculum
- Create and initiate hands-on learning experiences
- Design and implement integrated learning centers
- Advise and counsel parents on their child's specific cognitive or emotional problems
- Coordinate with other teachers on special school programs

EMPLOYMENT HISTORY

Third Grade Teacher, Briggs Elementary School, Frankfort, PA (September 1985 - current)
- Created and implemented "Guest Reader" program, where local officials and business people visit the classroom to read books to the students, building a positive relationship between the school and community and introducing students to civic leaders
- Developed learning center on dinosaurs for first- through third-grade students, which earned State Teacher's Association recognition for combining math, history and science in a primary school project
- Helped coordinate and implement home/school electronic mail network, which allows parents and teachers to communicate via computer to verify homework assignments, follow up on previous communication and discuss a student's progress; network has resulted in increased parent communication and classroom participation and improved school work among students
- Coordinate annual school Christmas program and all third-grade field trips

Kindergarten Teacher, Warren Elementary School, Williamsburg, PA (September 1983 - June 1985)
- Secured grant for classroom computer and created computer learning center, which introduced students to computers and prepared them for future school assignments
- Initiated special classroom projects, resulting in increased parent participation in the classroom
- Created "Animals in our World" program, which introduced students to rare and endangered animals and their habitats

Substitute Teacher, Warren County School Corporation, Williamsburg, PA (October 1982 - June 1983)
- Guided students (elementary through high school) through lessons set by teacher
- Served on team that created substitute teacher manual, resulting in standardized procedures for common classroom situations and problems

(continued)

EMPLOYMENT HISTORY

Student Teacher, Washington Elementary School, Washington, PA (February 1982 - May 1982)
- Worked two months with kindergarten students and two months in a third-grade classroom
- Modified lessons for and streamlined two learning-disabled children into regular curriculum
- Created reading center for third-grade classroom, which provided activities and reading materials for students who finished their school work before others
- Assisted in after-school tutor program

Teaching Assistant, Lil Tikes Nursery School, Washington, PA (September 1979 - January 1982)
- Stimulated the creativity in children through various art and creative dance projects
- Guided children through problems by positive verbal and nonverbal interactions
- Initiated role playing as a way to learn to solve problems

Swimming Instructor, YMCA, Washington, PA (Summers 1975 - current)
- Instruct children ages two to 14 in beginning and intermediate swimming and water safety skills
- Work with 150 children each summer

EDUCATION

Bachelor of Science Degree, Early Childhood Education, Pennsylvania State University, *with honors* (1978)

EDUCATIONAL ACTIVITIES

Cheevers County Community School System
- Parents' Council, CHANGE (Community Helping Answer a Need for Greater Education) Committee
- Secretary, Elementary School Improvement Team

State Computers in the Classroom Association (past president, current committee chair)

OTHER INSTRUCTIONAL ACTIVITIES

Sunday School teacher, St. Thomas Church, Williamsburg, PA
Leader for Child Care 4-H Project, Cheevers County, PA
Little League Coach, Williamsburg, PA

LOUISE T. SHEPHERD
910 Crescent Dr.
Marion, NV 89113
(702) 555-0173

SKILLS PROFILE

- Five years experience teaching special education students.
- Certified in instructing the emotionally handicapped, learning disabled and mildly mentally handicapped.
- Experienced in placing eligible special education students in regular classrooms.
- Skilled in developing and improving students' social skills and successfully addressing behavioral problems.
- Adept in conducting case conferences and working with parents.

EMPLOYMENT HISTORY

Williams County School District, Marion, NV

Special Services Teacher, Lincoln High School (Sept 1993-current)
Instruct up to 10 emotionally handicapped (EH), learning disabled (LD) and mildly mentally handicapped (MIMH) students. Work with MIMH and EH students in self-contained classroom and place eligible LD students in regular classrooms through inclusionary program.

- Develop individualized lesson plans for each student in self-contained classroom.
- Implemented inclusionary program and guide general education teachers in modifying curriculum to address special education students' abilities.
- Assisted four MIMH students in earning passing grades in regular biology.
- Developed and implemented Individual Evaluation Program, which requires teacher of record to write individual evaluations on each student and share results with parents.

Teaching Assistant, Lincoln High School (Sept 1991-June 1993)
Assisted special services staff with students at various learning levels (MIMH, EH, LD). Assisted general education teachers in modifying lessons. Created curriculum for special education students grades 9-11. Counseled students on behavioral and social problems.

- Instructed inclusionary classes in English and physical science.
- Worked one-on-one with three MIMH students, evaluated their progress and conducted parent conferences.

(continued)

WORK EXPERIENCE

Williams County School District, Marion, NV

Homebound Tutor (Sept 1991-June 1993)
Created curriculum in all areas for two middle school and two high school students (MIMH, EH). Counseled students on behavioral and emotional issues.

Pine City Community School Corporation, Pine City, NV

Student Teacher, Pine City High School (Jan - March 1991)
Worked eight weeks with general education students and eight weeks with special education students in grades 9-12. Designed various lesson plans and coordinated several unit plans. Assisted general education teachers in modifying lesson plans for special education students.

- Worked one-on-one with three LD and EH students in self-contained classroom and guided and assisted one LD student in regular classrooms.

EDUCATION/CERTIFICATION

Bachelor of Science, University of Nevada, Carson City (1991)
Major: Special Education
Minor: Secondary Education

Certified Instructor, LD/EH/MIMH, University of Nevada, Carson City (1992)

EDUCATIONAL MEMBERSHIPS

Member, Nevada Association of Special Education Teachers
Member, Fundraising Committee, Williams County Education Foundation

ACTIVITIES

Volunteer, Marion Public Library, Marion, NV

Kevin C. Myers
1112 Somerset Ct.
Burlington, VT 05406
(802) 555-6223

Skills Profile

More than 20 years of teaching and administrative experience. Skilled in encouraging and supporting restructuring efforts and moving the decision-making process closer to the classroom. Solid background in developing a variety of learning environments that actively engage students.

Work Experience

July 1989-current

Superintendent of Schools, Burlington Community School Corporation, Burlington, VT

- Initiated and implemented several school reform projects, including year-round school education (1994), and the only integrated, thematic elementary school in the eastern third of the country (1993).
- Earned Smithton Award for Innovation in Education (1994).
- Spearheaded several district-wide technology projects, including integrating computer technology and video information systems and implementing long-distance interactive learning programs at high-school level.
- Initiated and implemented two building renovation programs, averaging $25M each.
- Worked with staff and school board members in multi-faceted, professional development program based on effective school research.

July 1983-July 1989

Assistant Superintendent of Schools, Montpelier Community School Corporation, Montpelier, VT

- Managed business operations and fiscal services.
- Handled teacher collective bargaining, district budget preparation and contract management.
- Developed alternative learning programs for at-risk students grades K-12, which successfully oriented them to the learning process.
- Promoted and facilitated funded grant proposals, with revenue exceeding $1M in six years, resulting in innovative curricular programs.

June 1981-July 1983

Director of Instruction and Curriculum, Montpelier Community School Corporation, Montpelier, VT

- Supervised curriculum development and management of K-12 instructional programs.
- Revised and modified achievement testing and formative evaluation of all instructional programs for the corporation, which better reflected students' progress in innovative curriculum.

(continued)

Work Experience

June 1979-June 1981   **Building Level Administrator,** Brackett Middle School, Richmond Community School System, Richmond, VA
- Managed all activities in 1,200-student, open-spaced middle school (grades 6-8).
- Implemented differential staffing model, using instructional assistants and teacher interns.

August 1974-June 1979   **Classroom Teacher,** Richmond Community School System, Richmond, VA
- Instructed eighth- and ninth-grade classes in chemistry and biology.
- Developed instructional television project, involving programming for biological sciences.

Education   Doctorate of Education, University of Vermont, Montpelier (1983)
Educational Specialist Degree, University of Virginia, Richmond (1980)
Master of Arts in Education, University of Virginia, Richmond (1976)
Bachelor of Arts in Biology, University of Virginia, Richmond (1974)

Licensing   Vermont - Superintendent (Professional)
Virginia - State Teacher, Superintendent

Professional Activities   Member, American Association of School Administrators
Member, Association of Supervision and Curriculum Development
Member, Vermont Association of Public School Superintendents
Member, Vermont Association of School Business Officials
Member, State Education Task Force
- Designed new Principal Preparation Model
- Developed state's Center for Creativity

Community Activities   Treasurer, Tri-County Mental Health Association
Member, Rotary Club

ELISABETH GARCIA
932 S. Woodrow Lane
Atlanta, GA 30128
(404) 555-2993

**SUMMARY OF
QUALIFICATIONS**

- Licensed professional engineer with nearly 10 years experience completing multi-million dollar construction projects
- Able to monitor, update and successfully meet construction schedules and finish at or under budget
- Capable of sequencing work to maintain existing operations
- Skilled in project budgeting and cost analysis with excellent background in estimating
- Experienced in bidding and contracting construction work

**PROFESSIONAL
EXPERIENCE**

Williams Mathau, Inc., Atlanta, GA

Project Manager (1992-current)
- Managed construction of a $135M, 520,000-sf research facility for a major pharmaceuticals firm
- Developed and implemented new bidding procedure that resulted in 15% more contracts
- Successfully bid/contracted more than $90M of work
- Serve as trainer for in-house seminars on time management and procedures

Project Manager (1991-1992)
- Managed construction of a $20M, 1,500-space parking structure for major research firm
- Performed cost/design analysis of post-tension CIP and precast microsilica structural frames
- Supervised engineering team of 15

Assistant Project Manager (1990-1991)
- Managed construction of $5.5 million underground pedestrian connector for major research center
- Successfully sequenced work across major roadway, resulting in uninterrupted traffic flow and minimal construction congestion
- Initiated project procedures for contractors and staff, which reduced submittals and enhanced completion of project time line

(continued)

PROFESSIONAL
EXPERIENCE

Miles & McGill Co., Houston, TX

Project Engineer (1988-1990)
- Served as engineer on $16M, 85,000-sf concourse and $18M, 1,500-space parking structure for Houston Airport Authority
- Handled all project schedule monitoring/updating
- Expedited submittals and materials to complete project ahead of schedule

Project Engineer (1987-1988)
- Served as project engineer on $2.5M utility relocation program for major research facility
- Relocated chilled water mains, purified water and high voltage electrical feeds
- Sequenced work to maintain existing plant operations, allowing plant staff to complete projects on schedule and meet customer needs, unaffected by construction progress

Assistant Project Engineer (1986)
- Served as assistant engineer on a $15M, 100,000-sf printing press facility
- Handled weekly schedule monitoring/updating
- Expedited fabrication and delivery of materials to ensure timely project completion

Scheduling and Estimating Training, Manager of Scheduling (1984-1986)
- Performed quantity take-offs and data base estimating
- Promoted to Manager of Scheduling after one year

EDUCATION/
LICENSING

Licensed Professional Engineer in the State of Georgia (1991)
Masters of Science Degree in Civil Engineering, Texas A&M (1985)
Bachelor of Science Degree in Construction Management Engineering, Purdue University, West Lafayette, IN (1984)

MEMBERSHIPS

District Officer, Georgia Chapter of ASCE (1992-current)
Chairman, St. Joseph's Church Building Committee (1991-current)
- Managed $.5M building expansion, finishing it on schedule and on budget

GARY SANDERS
4506 N. Vernon St.
Tecumseh, WI 53225
(414) 555-9203

Profile:

Professional engineer with more than 15 years of experience in rural and municipal electric operations. Excellent supervision and labor relations. Ability to design and successfully implement cost-saving and service-improving procedures. Skilled in system planning, preventive maintenance, budget management and designing standardized procedures and training programs.

Work Experience:
March 1989-present

Engineering Manager, Madison County Rural Electric, Tecumseh, WI
Handle system planning, design, metering, substation maintenance and provide technical consultation. Supervise four employees. Direct day-to-day, annual and long-term engineering and planning.
- Coordinated program that reduced maintenance overtime, enhanced system reliability during major system disruptions and reduced outage times for all nine substations
- Managed peak-controlling equipment installation and start-up, which resulted in annual savings of nearly $200,000
- Designed, developed, constructed and installed voltage control equipment for six substations for a total installed cost of under $1,000 each
- Produced work plans for REA approval and budgetary purposes and directed return to standard REA construction specifications for all construction projects
- Produced the first set of company-wide job descriptions with associated organizational chart
- Handled economic evaluation of various projects, such as diesel engines for trucks and low-loss transformers

1984-1989

Assistant Manager, Albion Power & Light, Albion, WI
Supervised three departments and 45 employees for 6,000-meter company with $3.5 million annual sales.
- Assisted manager in reducing nearly $500,000 power bill indebtedness to 2 percent positive margin in two years
- Closed out-of-date, high-cost generation station while increasing financial margins and maintaining full employment for all 40 employees
- Assisted manager in reorganizing operation, including new job descriptions and responsibilities for power plant, distribution and office personnel in a union environment

(continued)

Work Experience:

1984-1989

Assistant Manager, Albion Power & Light, Albion, WI
Organized preventive maintenance program. Researched programs for future power supplies.
- Designed and implemented various standardized procedures and training programs, which reduced procedural errors
- Oversaw clerical help handling billing, cash receipts, accounts receivable and payable, auditing, and general record keeping
- Initiated and completed change over to computerized billing system, which reduced a three-month back log

1980-1984

Staff Engineer, Morrow and Company, Walters, WI
Coordinated and managed major repair and maintenance projects up to $750,000.
- Designed and implemented preventive maintenance program for major power substation and distribution facilities
- Recommended and designed new training program, which reduced procedural errors

1978-1980

Substation Designer, Cooperative Education Student, Public Service Wisconsin, Madison, WI
- Completed design projects as assigned by staff engineer
- Assisted in standardizing training manuals, enhancing engineering operations
- Gained experience supervising and working with union employees

Education:

1980

B.S. in Electrical Engineering Technology, *with honors*, Wisconsin State University

Memberships:

1982-present

American Association of Electrical Engineers

1990-present

Advisor, Wisconsin State University Association of Student Engineers

Related Activities:

1993-present

Project Leader, 4-H Electronics Project, Madison County 4-H, Tecumseh, WI

Jeanette D. McCann, Ph.D.
33 Westview Dr.
Wilmington, DE 19899
(302) 555-3994

PROFILE   Skilled technical manager with doctorate in materials and more than six years of project management experience. Excellent background in planning and directing technical efforts, in manufacturing process development and in product improvement programs. Strong analytical and investigative skills.

PROFESSIONAL EXPERIENCE

October 1989 - current   **Willow Technical Systems, Wilmington, DE**

Senior Materials Engineer

Direct all technical activity on internally funded multi-year product development/process optimization programs. Forecast, budget and schedule program milestones for all programs. Manage annual program budget of more than $800,000. Supervise nine engineers.

- Serve as in-house focal point for materials and processing issues and establish procedures that enhance production coordination and increase productivity.
- Serve as project engineer for customer and government-funded materials/process development programs and coordinate engineering functions to successfully meet customer schedule and budget requirements.
- Established coordination components for company-wide functions, which help move projects toward defined goals and enhance ability to meet customer needs, budgets and schedules.
- Revised application of high-strength steels, advanced aluminum alloys, metal and polymer composites and ceramics in aerospace products, resulting in improved product performance and increased sales.
- Developed process that concentrated on casting methods, thermal and mechanical treatments, powder metallurgy, joining methods and machining and grinding, which provided the opportunity to develop new products and markets.
- Directed high-performance material assessment, including material characterization for design, damage tolerance and fracture mechanics, which improved manufacturing process and product development.

(continued)

PROFESSIONAL EXPERIENCE

May 1986 - October 1989   **Mayfair Incorporated, Wilmington, DE**

Research Engineer

Managed projects for several externally sponsored and company-funded manufacturing development programs. Presented program highlights at executive conferences and trade shows.

- Emphasized the material's influence on optimal processing methods, resulting in improved manufacturing processes and products.
- Handled the entire spectrum of the traditional material removal processes, nonconventional techniques, tool design, process design and expert systems.
- Revised research process to better coordinate with product marketing, resulting in more successful marketing programs and increased sales.

EDUCATION

Doctorate of Materials Science and Engineering, University of Delaware (1987)
Dissertation topic: Alloy modifications to Deotel 61 to reduce additions of strategic elements while retaining the original material properties.

Master of Science, University of Delaware (1985)
Thesis topic: Optimizing the structure and properties of advanced cast irons to improve thermal fatigue resistance.

Bachelor of Science, University of Delaware (1983)

PUBLICATIONS

Doctoral Dissertation
McCann, *Metallurgy and Properties Research*, Pressman Publishers, 1990.

Master's Thesis
McCann, *National Foundryman's Journal*, Wolcott & Associates, 1986.

Invited Papers/Presentations
"Cutting Tool Geometry Effects on the Machining of Aerospace Materials"
1990 International Machine Tool Show, Chicago, IL

"Composite Materials in Torpedo Propulsion Systems"
1995 American Defense Preparedness Association, Colorado Springs, CO

Dennis K. Ruddell • 6521 N. County Line Rd. • Gaithersburg, IL • 60221 • (708) 555-3551

Summary of Qualifications

Extensive background in rural housing and agricultural loans, appraisal and financial planning. Skilled in developing loan packages with sound financial plans, realistic cash flows and proper security. Experienced in public administration and handling government contracts. Adept in communicating information about government programs to the public. Excellent supervisory, organizational, analytical and computer skills.

Work Experience

Agricultural Management Specialist-County Supervisor, United States Department of Agriculture-Farmers Home Administration:

Gaithersburg, IL (June 1992-current)
Wawaset, IL (Oct 1990-June 1992)

- Approve loans up to $360,000
- Properly manage, service and maintain loan portfolio of approximately $32 million representing 90 farm and 410 housing borrowers
- Work with delinquent and insolvent borrowers to defer, reschedule, re-amortize, consolidate, write down or liquidate loans
- Cooperate with other lending institutions on subordinations, releases and FmHA guaranteed loans
- Manage acquired property involving maintenance, repair, lease and sale, usually through government contracts
- Manage office and seven-person staff covering six central Illinois counties
- Initiated and received department/government approval to upgrade computer system and software, resulting in easier information retrieval and analysis and more informative financial report generation

Agricultural Assistant to the County Supervisor, United States Department of Agriculture Farmers Home Administration, Mulberry, IL

(March 1988-Oct 1990)

- Recommended for approval and serviced rural housing and agricultural loans
- Appraised real and chattel security property
- Implemented new government program for borrowers involved in bankruptcy proceedings, resulting in faster closings, less paper work and less government contract work
- Initiated quarterly meetings with local farmers and agribusiness representatives to explain changes in state and federal laws and regulations, enhancing customer service and enabling farm owners/operators to establish successful businesses

Assistant Farm Manager and Rural Appraiser, Taylor Land Services, Springfield, Illinois

(June 1986-March 1988)

- Assisted in farm management
- Handled preliminary preparation of rural real estate appraisals
- Assisted in accounting, payables, receivables, bookkeeping, payroll and preparation of technical documents and reports
- Recommended updated accounting system, which provided a more customer-oriented financial analysis, enhancing customer service

(continued)

Work Experience

Student Staff Assistant, University of Illinois, Vocational Agriculture Services, Urbana, Illinois
(Aug 1983-May 1986)
- Assisted in billing and record-keeping
- Developed microcomputer programs for accounting and office purposes, resulting in more accurate bookkeeping and improved analysis
- Worked in all areas of agriculture through sales and production of agricultural education materials

Integrated Pest Management Scout, Warren County Cooperative Extension, Westfield, Ohio
(Summer 1986)
- Solely responsible for scouting 35 farms in central Ohio
- Checked corn, soybean and alfalfa fields for insect, weed and disease damage, and completed soil and tissue sampling and testing
- Reported findings to farmers and Extension Service

Education

Bachelor of Science Degree in Agricultural Economics (1986)
University of Illinois, College of Agriculture, Urbana, Illinois

Honors

- FmHA County Office of the Year (1992)
- FmHA Certificate of Outstanding Accomplishment (1991)
- FmHA Certificate of Merit (1990)
- Administrative Point of Light for Community Service with Farm Safety for Just Kids Program (1991)

Volunteer Activities

Organizing Director, Green County Farm Safety for Just Kids Day Camp
(1992-current)
- Established farm safety program for children, including presentations from local law enforcement and emergency medical services, farm owners/operators and agricultural chemical representatives
- Handle all public relations and coordinate up to 25 volunteers
- Secure sponsorships so program can be offered free-of-charge to participants

Other Affiliations

President, Optimist Club of Gaithersburg (1994-current)
Treasurer, Green County Young Farmers (1993-current)

Amanda Woodfield
19 E. Lansing Dr.
Tidewater, VA 23033
(804) 555-2993

Skills Summary

Pharmacist with more than 10 years of experience, including extensive background in administering government programs. Skilled in developing record-keeping and patient profile systems and creating in-service training programs. Experienced in preparing budgets and monthly department reports. Experienced in serving as consultant to various medical staffs on medication interactions, adverse effects and appropriate dosages.

Employment

Pharmacist, Industrial Rehabilitation Center, Virginia Bureau of Worker's Compensation, Tidewater, VA (1993-current)

Accurately order and distribute medications to clients and provide client counseling in accordance with VBRA 40. Develop and implement wean schedules for clients, helping them to reduce and eventually eliminate medication use. Prepare and conduct in-service training for staff. Prepare fiscal year budget and monthly reports.

- Developed record-keeping system for pharmacy, including new forms for tracking medication received, distributed and returned, resulting in more accurate records and improved inventory control.
- Created new patient profile system for pharmacy, which allowed for review of accurate, up-to-date patient profiles to determine medication interactions, adverse effects and appropriate dosages.
- Established physician signature card process, reducing physician approval delays by 35%.
- Created protocol for contingency cabinet, which established detailed operating procedures and eliminated unwarranted use.

(continued)

**Pharmacist, Support Services, Virginia Department of Mental Health, Tidewater, VA
(1989-1993)**

Accurately dispensed psychotropic medication to outpatient mental health agencies throughout Virginia in a timely manner. Reviewed patient profiles for medication interactions, adverse effects, and appropriate dosages using both manual and computerized processing system.

- Supervised final phase of data entry from manual to computerized system, resulting in increased productivity, improved record keeping and enhanced inventory summaries.
- Initiated and conducted training sessions covering changes in state and federal pharmacy laws and newly marketed medications, ensuring compliance and resulting in a well-informed staff.
- Maintained well-controlled inventory, including legally handling and storing controlled substances.

**Staff Pharmacist, Nursing Center Services, Virginia Department of Mental Health, Tidewater, VA
(1986-1989)**

Accepted and transcribed physician medication orders submitted by telephone from nursing home nursing staff. Checked and accurately dispensed, in a timely fashion, medication filled by pharmacy technicians.

- Checked unit dose medication packages for correct medication and legal labeling.
- Checked narcotic unit dose packages for legal labeling and storage according to Virginia state law.
- Created information packet concerning medication dosages, adverse effects and interactions to help answer questions from nursing home staff, resulting in a well-informed staff and increased productivity for pharmacy.

Staff Pharmacist, Green County Memorial Hospital, Greenville, VA (1984-1986)

Accurately dispensed unit dose medication according to physician orders. Maintained patient profiles with emphasis on drug interactions and dosages.

- Answered questions from medical staff concerning drug dosages, interactions and adverse effects.
- Implemented new unit dose medication system for hospital, resulting in increased productivity and more timely delivery of medications.

Education

Bachelor of Science, Pharmacy (1984)
Virginia State University
Columbus, VA

JANET W. ENGLISH

4460 Parker Road
Livonia, Mich. 48152

(313) 555-3553

SUMMARY OF SKILLS

Registered nurse with solid background in health education and social work. Skilled in developing programs and services that directly address community needs and achieve desired results. Experienced in working with community leaders and government agencies to successfully implement programs.

WORK EXPERIENCE

June 1989-current   **St. Elizabeth Hospital, Detroit, Mich.**

Community Outreach Manager (October 1994-current)
Manage neighborhood office, which provides educational services and works to improve living conditions for 2,000 of city's poorest citizens in run-down housing project. Secure grants to fund services and programs. Coordinate work with variety of community and government agencies. Supervise two-member staff.
- Established Resident's Council and led community survey, which determined resident's needs and goals.
- Worked with council and other agencies, including Housing and Urban Development (HUD), to secure grants and build affordable housing for area residents, with June 1996 projected completion date.
- Create and direct family and youth programs, which have reduced area vandalism and juvenile crime.
- Plan and supervise variety of educational and job-training programs, which provide residents with needed information and skills.
- Currently working on program to reduce infant mortality rate by establishing neighborhood store where mothers may "purchase" maternity and baby items with coupons received for obtaining pre-natal and well-baby care.

(continued)

WORK EXPERIENCE

Community Outreach Coordinator (April 1992-October 1994)
Managed outreach program that works with community leaders and residents to care for emotionally, spiritually, medically and financially needy residents. Managed budget and two staff members.
- Supervised survey to determine needs of rural community and developed necessary resources and staff to address identified issues.
- Worked with community to establish co-operative day care, which provides quality child care and helps adults develop job skills and learn good parenting skills.
- Developed mobile health program, staffed by hospital medical residents, to provide pre-natal and well-baby care.
- Created referral system with cooperation from local ministerial board, school system, physicians and county offices, which helps residents secure needed services.
- Initiated and implemented hearing and health screenings in local festivals and fairs that target the elderly and determine their health care needs.

GYN/Oncology RN (June 1989-April 1992)
Cared for routine GYN post-surgery patients and GYN oncology patients. Administered chemotherapy and cared for routine post-partum and C-section patients.
- Earned 1991 Quality Care Award.

EDUCATION

June 1989   B.S. in Nursing, University of Michigan, Ann Arbor

ACTIVITIES

Volunteer Educator, Campaign for Healthy Babies, Detroit

THERESA A. LUTZ
51 N. Black Hill Dr.
Rapid City, S.D. 57709
(605) 555-9883

PROFILE

- Nearly 10 years experience in developing community resources, recruiting professional and volunteer personnel and operating efficiently and effectively within budget constraints.
- Solid background in securing grants from proposal stage through reporting on compliance and financial issues.
- Effective public relations skills, including delivering formal presentations, written communications, and planning and conducting fund-raising campaigns.

WORK EXPERIENCE

Executive Director, Sioux County Senior Services, Inc., Black Hills, S.D. (August 1988-present)
Supervise organization's service program and daily operations. Work closely with board of directors and carry out policies and programs. Supervise five full-time and 10 part-time staff. Develop programs, solicit funds, recruit board members and train staff members. Oversee two annual fund-raising events.

- Formed not-for-profit entity in 1988 to coordinate needed senior services.
- Built organization into valuable service provider with more than 275 volunteers who offer up to 20 services (such as homemaking, home health care, and tax and insurance assistance) to more than 2,500 seniors in the community.
- Prepare federal, state and private grant proposals with high record of acceptance.
- Plan and administer $325,000 annual budget.
- Established respite care program, which provides relief to family members caring for homebound seniors through qualified volunteers.

Volunteer Coordinator, Arrow County Senior Services, Elgin, Wyo. (Oct 1986-June 1988)
Worked with and scheduled up to 150 volunteers annually to provide variety of services to county's senior citizens. Edited "50 plus" section in local newspaper.

- Secured donated vehicles and scheduled volunteer drivers to establish transportation service.
- Implemented hearing and health screenings for seniors at local fairs and festivals.
- Implemented organization's first Christmas tree fund raiser, which realized nearly $2,000 in profit annually.
- Increased number of volunteers 75% during tenure.
- Established referral system for seniors in need of counseling, tax assistance, insurance assistance and more.

(continued)

WORK EXPERIENCE

Second Grade Teacher, Elgin Public Schools, Elgin, Wyo. (Sept 1984-June 1988)

Provided appropriate curriculum, guidance and hands-on experiences for 22 children. Provided regular feedback to parents on children's progress. Coordinated and scheduled all field trips for four second- and third-grade classes.

- Worked with administration to establish new guidelines for textbook selection, which improved quality of materials in elementary education classrooms.
- Created volunteer pool to assist with math and reading tutoring during classroom hours, which provided additional assistance to students and increased parental involvement.
- Researched adding computers to elementary education classrooms and helped plan September 1988 implementation.

EDUCATION/CERTIFICATION

B.S. in Elementary Education, Wyoming University, Cheyenne (1984)

Counseling Courses, South Dakota University, Rapid City (1990-1992)

Certified Home Economist in Human Services (1989)

ACTIVITIES

President, Zonta International Businesswomen's Association, Rapid City, S.D.

Volunteer, Rapid City Children's Choir

John L. Martin

951 Ford Rd.
Alexandria, VA 22392
(703) 555-2442

Summary of Qualifications

- Seven years experience in constituent relations, legislative research and evaluation.
- Solid background in public event planning, scheduling and coordination.
- Skilled in researching and preparing issue- and event-related briefing material.
- Experienced in campaign management, including successful fund-raising programs.

Work Experience

Legislative Assistant, U.S. Senator Steven Knight of Massachusetts, Washington, DC
(May 1994-current)
Serve as liaison between Senator Knight and constituents on agriculturally related legislation.
- Manage agricultural-specific projects and draft comprehensive reviews of projects and legislation.
- Established "town meetings" between Senator and constituents, which provide input and insight into current issues and concerns.
- Manage constituent correspondence and arrange tours of Capitol.

Advanceman, Governor William Tollifson, State of Massachusetts, Boston
(November 1992-May 1994)
Traveled with governor to all public events and maintained governor's schedule.
- Compiled information about top concerns and issues for each locale/event.
- Managed constituent requests and prepared follow-up correspondence.

Campaign Staff, William Tollifson for Governor, Boston
(May 1991-November 1992)
- Chaired fund-raising committee, which increased number of donors from 2,000 to 12,000 and raised more than $2 million in campaign contributions through direct solicitation, direct mail, events and receptions.
- Assisted in volunteer coordination.

Schedule Coordinator, Massachusetts Democratic State Committee, Boston
(September 1989-May 1991)
Coordinated public events schedules for four state candidates and office holders.
- Prospected events for candidates, which increased their visibility and enhanced their public image.
- Organized and directed five-day, 30-city campaign bus tour.

Legislative/Administrative Intern, Massachusetts Trial Lawyers Association (MTLA), Boston, MA
(June 1988-September 1989)
- Maintained and updated computerized and hard-copy records of more than 500 pieces of legislation.
- Analyzed and evaluated more than 1,000 pages of legal decisions, statutes and civil codes.
- Prepared evaluations and reports for House and Senate committees and the MTLA Board of Directors.

Education

Bachelor of Arts in Political Science, Massachusetts University, Boston (1988)

ANNA WHITE CLOUD

(After June 15, 1996)
154 Columbia St.
Sierra, NM 87002
(505) 555-4667

(Until June 15, 1996)
519 University St., #3B
Albuquerque, NM 87112
(505) 555-1992

SKILLS SUMMARY

Solid background in environmental and wildlife education. Skilled in
working with the public and increasing understanding of ecological issues.
Experienced in maintaining park facilities and trails. Fluent in Spanish.

EXPERIENCE

Sept 1995-current

Recreation Management Intern
High Sierra Forest Preserve, NM
Provide visitors with information on ecology, environmental resources and
forest management. Lead guided tours and informative discussions on
environmental issues.
* Developed and present educational program on wildlife habitats.
* Created new walking trail, which provides visitors with guided tour to
  tracking wildlife.

June 1992-Aug 1995

Volunteer/Summer Intern
Apache National Forest, NM
Met visitors at Visitor's Center, answered questions and provided trail maps.
Assisted forest rangers in inspecting and maintaining public facilities,
shelters, trail markers and monuments.
* Helped develop new educational program on wildlife management for
  Visitor's Center.
* Designed new trail map, which coordinated with color-coded trail markers
  and explained degrees of hiking difficulty.

EDUCATION

Bachelor of Science in Recreation Management, University of New Mexico,
Albuquerque (Expected June 1996)
Related course work: environmental resources, biology, ecology, park
management, recreational resource planning and public relations.

ACTIVITIES

Volunteer, Museum of Native American Culture, Albuquerque, NM

Jeanne D. Temple

905 Edgewood Dr.
Prairie, ID 70012
(902) 555-1044

Summary of Qualifications

- Eight years experience in park and recreation management, including implementing creative programs to increase interest in the park and benefit the community.
- Solid background in facilities management and maintaining attractive park grounds.
- Skilled administrator with experience in fund raising and budget management.

Work Experience

Parks Director, Prairie Parks System, Prairie, ID (September 1990-present)

Manage two community parks and six employees. Chair board of directors and oversee $400,000 budget. Monitor and enhance ecological aspects of park.

- Initiated and implemented variety of new programs, such as photography contest, Easter egg hunt, summer community band concerts, Haunted Trail, hayrides and annual volleyball tournament, which have increased participation in park activities.
- Secured funding and managed $125,000 building expansion, which provides new baseball park press box and improved protection for maintenance and playground equipment.
- Established "Trees to Remember" program, which allows residents to donate trees as memorials and enhances park's ecological balance.
- Worked with civic organizations and Boise Symphony Orchestra to establish "Symphony at Sunset at Prairie Park," which draws people to park, provides cultural opportunity and enhances orchestra's visibility in rural area.

Assistant Parks Director, Glendale Park System, Glendale, ID
(June 1987-September 1990)

Developed educational programs and supervised grounds-keeping and picnic shelters for four-park system.

- Supervised park swimming pool renovation, which finished one week ahead of schedule and $10,000 under budget.
- Worked with athletic trainer to develop park fitness walk, which provided educational material and suggested exercise programs for a variety of age and ability levels.
- Initiated and conducted summer camps, which included teaching school-age children about ecology and biology to increase their interest in the sciences.

Biology Teacher, Glendale Community School Corp., Glendale, ID
(September 1985-June 1987)

Instructed junior high and high school students in biology and general science.

- Designed ecological learning center and outdoor lab, which provided students with opportunity to study relationships between living things and their environments.

Education/Licensing

Bachelor of Science in Biology, University of Idaho, Boise (1985)
　Minor: Horticulture
Idaho State Teaching License (1985)

Nancy Stetson • 45 Valley Ridge Rd. • Willow, NE • 68023 • (402) 555-9203

Summary of Qualifications

Nearly 10 years experience in social work, including administration, supervision and training. Excellent background in assisting emotionally/behaviorally disturbed children and their families. Experienced in developing and implementing treatment plans and services and working with the community, local referral agencies and school systems. Skilled in fund raising and event planning. Accustomed to successfully juggling several responsibilities simultaneously.

Work Experience

Admissions Social Worker, Nebraska Lutheran Children's Home, Willow, NE
(November 1993 - current)

Receive and coordinate referrals for admissions to the agency. Schedule and conduct pre-admission and diagnostic assessments. Serve as liaison with referral sources such as the County Division of Family and Children/Welfare, courts, parents and schools.

- Schedule and conduct in-service training for various staff, including child care workers, social workers and on-grounds school teachers.
- Serve as co-leader for treatment groups, including anger management, survivors of molestation and children of alcoholics.
- Worked with local church music department to create choir from children's home; choir performs monthly during worship service; membership has grown from 15 to 42; social workers have documented increased self-esteem and improved group interaction skills among choir members.
- Assisted public relations manager in revising annual fund raiser used with Lutheran churches across the country, which resulted in a 20% increase in donations.

Social Worker, Nebraska Lutheran Children's Home, Willow, NE
(April 1989 - November 1993)

Developed and implemented treatment plans and services for emotionally/behaviorally disturbed girls and their families. Provided written and verbal progress reports to placing agencies, including testifying at court hearings. Provided individual, group and family counseling.

- Worked with families to determine appropriate communication and limit-setting in the home.
- Met with public school personnel to assess residents' ongoing educational needs.
- Organized and chaired for three years an auction of goods donated from local businesses and community residents, which raised more than $10,000 annually.

Child Care Worker, Smithton Home for Girls, Rockville, NE
(June 1986 - April 1989)

Supervised daily activities of residents, including housekeeping, leisure and recreational time and study time. Observed residents' behavior, noting changes, significant incidents, both positive and negative.

- Established and maintained a working relationship with each resident's social worker.
- Created fund-raising event that brought in more than $2,500 annually.

Education/Certification

Bachelor of Arts, University of Nebraska, Lincoln (1986)
Majors: Psychology and Sociology

Certified Social Worker, State of Nebraska (1986)

REBECCA WILSON
45 Oak Drive
Wells, OH 43334
(419) 555-2667

Profile

Seasoned counselor and manager with training in–and insight into–human behavior, with special emphasis on addictive behavior and crisis intervention. Experienced in developing and directing counseling programs. Skilled in assessing patients and developing and administering treatment plans.

Professional Experience

May 1994 -current

Senior Outpatient Counselor, Center for Chemical Dependency, Memorial Hospital, Wells, OH
- Developed and implemented the center's first Domestic Violence Men's Group, enhancing the anger management and communication skills of abusers in a group setting
- Updated and revised eating disorder program to include prevention education for family and friends of patient, resulting in fewer reported cases and increased awareness among those groups
- Provide group after care counseling
- Conduct individual counseling of dual disorder (chemical dependency and mental illness) clients

Oct 1990-May 1994

Primary Case Manager, Bowen Counseling Center, Bedford, OH
- Served as Float Counselor in Intensive Psychiatric, Multi-Axis and Geroaddiction units
- Assessed clients and developed master treatment plans, objectives and methods
- Established guidelines for counselor discharge summaries to comply with insurance company requirements, resulting in faster claims results for patients and the center
- Organized four continuing education workshops, including hiring educators, securing classroom facilities, arranging lunches and providing necessary written materials
- Developed and implemented sibling awareness and prevention program for families of teenage patients in Alcohol Unit; 95% of the graduates continued to be alcohol-free one year after completing program

Feb 1986 -October 1990

Chaplain, Bowen Counseling Center, Bedford, OH
- Assessed patients and developed master treatment plans, involving chaplaincy goals, objectives and methods
- Led weekly grief/loss workshops, spirituality groups, step groups and individual and couples continuing care groups
- Established and led support group for couples who had lost an infant at birth
- Scheduled all chaplaincy events

(continued)

Volunteer Experience

Feb 1991-current   **Volunteer, Green County Caring Center, Wells, OH**
- Provide emotional counseling for six of the Caring Center's needy clients
- Refer all clients to appropriate county assistance agencies

March 1993-current   **Leader, Marriage Enrichment Program, Bedford Lutheran Church, Bedford, OH**
- Developed and currently lead community program housed by local church
- Created all lessons and written materials for program, which addresses and meets a community need

April 1985-Feb 1986   **Chaplaincy Internship, Green County Memorial Hospital, Waldon, OH**
- Completed educational process provided in cooperation with Christian Theological Seminary to experience all phases of the chaplain's role

Jan 1984-April 1985   **Volunteer, Ohio Women's Prison, Columbus, OH**
- Participated in crafts and conversation programs to enhance women's opportunities for positive interaction and increased self-esteem

Education

1990   Sacred Theology Masters in Pastoral Counseling, Christian Theological Seminary, Columbus, OH

1986   Master of Divinity, Christian Theological Seminary, Columbus, OH

1983   Bachelor of Science in Psychology, The Ohio State University, Columbus, OH

Certification/State Licensing

1990   Certified Alcoholism Counselor

1989   Certified Marriage and Family Therapist

Ordination

1986   Lutheran Church

Memberships

National Association of Pastoral Counselors
Ohio Association of Alcohol/Drug Abuse Counselors
Green County Council to Prevent Alcohol and Other Drug Abuse
Green County Task Force to Prevent Domestic Violence

JEFFREY D. FOUNDARY
703 Meadow View Rd., #24
Charleston, WV 25339
(304) 555-2992

SUMMARY OF QUALIFICATIONS

Exercise scientist with excellent experience in prescribing and supervising exercise programs, performing therapeutic modalities and conducting clinical exercise and health screening tests. Skilled in developing educational and training materials.

CLINICAL SKILLS/ABILITIES

- Perform rehabilitative modalities, including ultrasound, electrical stimulation, whirlpool, iontophoresis, paraffin and TENS unit
- Conduct work conditioning with BTE Work Simulator and LIDO Weight Machine
- Assess resting metabolic rate (Beckman Horizon Metabolic Cart) and resting electrocardiogram (Quinton ECG Cart)
- Test pulmonary functions with Puritan-Bennett, Gould Spirometer and Respirodyne II
- Test strength with Kin-Com III Isokinetic Dynamometer
- Assess body composition, including hydrostatic weighing with nitrogen analysis, Valhalla Medical 1990B Bio-Impedance, and skinfold calipers

PROFESSIONAL EXPERIENCE

Physical Abilities Testing Coordinator/Exercise Specialist, Methodist Hospital Industrial Rehabilitation Center, Charleston, WV (Sept 1995-current)

Implemented and market Physical Abilities Testing (PAT) Program. Organize and administer on-site job analysis, conduct physical abilities tests and administer PAT certification training sessions. Develop all necessary educational materials.
- Supervise work conditioning sessions, including orientation and instruction.
- Assist occupational therapist in hand clinic with rehabilitative therapy for acute and chronic injuries.
- Maintain and order equipment and therapy supplies.

Health Screening Specialist, Occupational Health Consulting Corporation, Charleston, WV (April 1993-Sept 1995)

Administered on-site corporate health screenings, including health risk assessment, flexibility and body composition. Organized staffing and scheduling for corporate health screenings.
- Developed and implemented screening protocols and educational materials.
- Initiated and developed staff training manual and training program.
- Conducted individual consultations with clients immediately following screenings.

(continued)

PROFESSIONAL EXPERIENCE

Exercise Specialist, The Fitness Center, Charleston, WV (June 1992-April 1993)
Administered exercise tests and fitness screenings, including graded exercise tests, muscular strength and endurance.
- Developed exercise prescriptions for clients.
- Recommended and created fitness screening manual, protocols and results handout, which provided necessary educational and follow-up information.

Exercise Specialist Intern, Center for Health and Fitness Services, Charleston, WV (March-June 1992)
Administered maximal and sub-maximal exercise tests and fitness assessments.
Developed exercise prescriptions and assisted with on-site health screenings.
- Presented fitness seminars to community groups, which helped educate the public about proper fitness and training.
- Participated in research project on exercise in older adults.

Student Athletic Trainer, West Virginia University, Wheeling, WV (Aug 1989-May 1992)
Performed treatment, preventive and rehabilitative techniques for acute and chronic athletic injuries.
- Served as physical therapy aid in University Hospital.

EDUCATION

B.S., Exercise Science/Counseling Psychology, West Virginia University, Wheeling (1992)

CERTIFICATIONS

- Certified CPR Rescuer/Community First Aid and Safety, American Red Cross
- Certified Ergonomic Specialist, Ergonomics, Inc.

AFFILIATIONS

- Member, American College of Sports Medicine

ACTIVITIES

- Weightlifting
- Marathon running

Claire E. Hudson
24 Stoneycreek Drive
Columbus, IL 61002
(815) 555-2934

Skills Profile

Professional with eight years experience in the health care industry, including marketing, project management, needs assessment and education. Experienced in developing programs and budgets, coordinating and training volunteers, and securing grants. Skilled in media and public relations, including creating brochures and writing press releases. Proficient in computer graphics software.

Work Experience

May 1993–current

Marketing Director, Center for Hand and Foot Surgery, Peoria, IL
Developed and maintain referral base of physicians and other health care providers. Develop annual work plan and budget for marketing areas. Orient new staff on office procedures and computerized scheduling system.
• Coordinate and negotiate contracts with managed care networks, resulting in an increased network of care-givers who must meet specific professional standards
• Developed tools for patient satisfaction and outcomes measurement, which has led to three new successful programs to address patient needs
• Serve as primary contact for all media-related and public-awareness projects
• Coordinate support groups and professional education seminars
• Produce flyers and brochures to inform patients and the public about the center's services, and educate the public about qualified health care

Feb 1990–May 1993

Vice President, Programs and Services, Multiple Sclerosis Foundation, Illinois Chapter, Peoria, IL
Developed annual objectives and budget for program-related areas. Hired and supervised program assistant. Served as primary contact for all media-related projects and press conferences.
• Designed new volunteer recruitment program, which increased the number of volunteers statewide by 40%
• Trained more than 200 volunteer instructors annually for MS programs
• Wrote and edited monthly press releases and quarterly newsletters
• Secured financial underwriting for projects, including annual telethon, which helped finance state education programs, free clinics and special events

Oct 1987–Feb 1990

Health Education Consultant, Crawford County Health Department, Westin, IL
• Secured grants for and coordinated community health needs assessment, which identified three major areas of concern
• Designed programs to address assessment needs and organized appropriate health education programs and volunteers throughout the county
• Conducted follow-up assessment, which found nearly 75% improvement in two of the identified areas and 55% improvement in the third

Education

B.A. in Public Health, University of Illinois, Urbana/Champaign, IL (1987)

OMKAR KHETTRY
921 Willow Lane
Mawtucket, CT 06323
(203) 555-7882

PROFILE

- MBA in Finance, HFMA Fellow (FHFMA) and Certified Manager of Patient Accounts
- Five years experience as hospital business office director
- Knowledgeable and skilled in working with hospital department managers, physicians and administration to improve bottom line
- Strong customer and patient relation skills

WORK EXPERIENCE

Business Office Director, Milton Memorial Hospital, Mawtucket, CT (June 1991-current)

Manage accounts receivable, insurance, collections, inpatient, outpatient and emergency room registrations, switchboard and all telephone system administration for 250-bed facility. Provide budgeting and cost reports assistance. Supervise and schedule up to 40 employees.
- Recommended new computer software, which provides more detailed patient information and allows hospital administrators to evaluate the need for current and future services.
- Established new collections policy, which increased collection of unpaid bills by 70%.
- Initiated new follow-up process with insurance companies, which has enhanced relations with carriers and patients and resulted in more timely payments to hospital.
- Honored for bringing office to highest production level ever in just two years.

Graduate Assistant, University of Connecticut School of Business, Danbury (August 1989-May 1991)

Provided class instruction for undergraduate students, including evaluating student projects and assigning final grades. Conducted research for professors.
- Assisted with School of Business career counseling program, which provided students with guidance in job searching, resume writing and job interviewing.
- Formed committee that reviewed and revised current undergraduate and graduate requirements to better prepare students for the job market.
- Named 1991 "Outstanding MBA Student" for contributions to MBA program.

EDUCATION

MBA in Finance, Cum Laude, University of Connecticut, Danbury, May 1991
BS in Marketing, Magna Cum Laude, University of Connecticut, Danbury, May 1989

PROFESSIONAL ORGANIZATIONS

Chairman, Healthcare Policy Committee, Eastern Chapter, Healthcare Financial Management Association, Danbury, CT (1993-present)
Board Member, Northeast Region, National Guild of Patient Account Managers (1994-current)

Rhonda Spencer • 16354 Dover Lane • Mountain Springs, CO • 80445 • (303) 555-9009

Summary of Qualifications

Award-winning registered nurse with strong background in supervision and all areas of patient care. Ten years' experience in CCU, ICU, medical and surgical progressive, general medical-surgical, orthopedics, home care and more. Also experienced in developing and implementing a variety of hospital patient care and employee training programs.

Work Experience

RN Case Manager, Home Health Services of General Hospital, Denver, CO
May 1993-current
- Manage total care needs for up to 30 patients (per week) in their homes.
- Supervise six Home Health Aides (HHAs).
- Plan and direct necessary additional training for aides, including annual CPR certification.
- Created brochure explaining hospital's home care program and how it benefits patients and their families, increasing number of clients by 35%.
- Developed and implemented hospital-based HHA training program to address demand for home aides, resulting in increased staff and increased opportunities to meet community needs.

Housewide Float RN, General Hospital, Denver, CO
October 1991-May 1993
- Quality care-giver in CCU, ICU, medical progressive, surgical progressive, general medical-surgical, orthopedics, post-partum, med-psych and newborn nursery.
- Revamped hospital's "New Mom/New Baby" patient information program and developed take-home package, which provided essential information and educational materials for new mothers on 24-hour stay.

General Post-Surgical RN, General Hospital, Denver, CO
December 1989-October 1991
- Cared for post-op patients, including EKG tracings, aerosol treatments and chest percussion, phlebotomy and lab test preparation, quality review and insurance recertification.

GYN/Oncology RN, Cooper Memorial Hospital, Colorado Springs, CO
November 1988-December 1989
- Cared for routine GYN post-surgery patients and GYN oncology patients.
- Administered chemotherapy and cared for routine post-partum and C-section patients.
- Developed hospital's "Family Care" support group program to address needs of family members of oncology patients, resulting in greater understanding of– and better ability to cope with–a terminally ill family member.

(continued)

Work Experience

CCU RN, Cooper Memorial Hospital, Colorado Springs, CO
August 1987-November 1989
- Handled basic and advanced EKG interpretation, care of pre- and post-catheterization patients, care of pre- and post-PTCA patients, intraortic balloon pump (IABP) monitoring, cardiac output monitoring, Swan Ganz catheter and arterial line care and monitoring, and pre- and post-coronary artery bypass graft (CABG) patients.

Emergency Department RN, Cooper Memorial Hospital, Colorado Springs, CO
May 1986-August 1987
- Helped develop program to familiarize probationary (still in training) firefighters and EMTs with emergency room procedures, resulting in better informed EMS staffs and enhancing emergency room operations.

CCU RN, Cooper Memorial Hospital, Colorado Springs, CO
May 1985-May 1986
- Served on committee that assessed patient visitation hours and wrote committee report to department head, which led to changes to better meet patient and family needs.

Student Nurse Extern, Colorado University Medical Center, Freemont, CO
December 1984-May 1985
- Cared for patients in all areas of the hospital.
- Delivered thank-you speech on behalf of all student nurses at annual hospital staff banquet.

Education/Certification
ANA Med-Surg Nursing Certificate (1989)
B.S. in Nursing, Colorado University, Freemont, CO (1986)
SON Diploma, Colorado University Medical Center, Freemont, CO (1982-1985)
General Studies, Mountain State University, Mountain Springs, CO (1981-1982)

Professional Organizations/Awards
1995	Secretary, Colorado Alliance for Home Health Care
1994	Outstanding RN Case Manager Award, General Hospital, Denver, CO
1993	Partner of the Year in Quality Care Award, General Hospital, Denver, CO

SUSAN MEREDITH
902 Vince Street
Lafayette, MT 59049
(406) 555-9091

OBJECTIVE   Expanded Duties Dental Assistant position in a private office or dental clinic.

SUMMARY OF QUALIFICATIONS

- Perform expanded duties such as rubber dam placement, pit and fissure sealants and Classes I, II, V amalgam restorations and Classes III, IV, V resin composite restorations
- Complete a variety of lab work, including custom trays, temporary crown, pouring and trimming models, trimming dies, plaster cast and stone dies
- Prepare tray set-ups and assist during procedures, including fillings and crown preps
- Clean and maintain X-ray processors, sterilize instruments
- Obtain and record patient information, including current treatment and conditions; code insurance forms

PROFESSIONAL EXPERIENCE

March 1994 - current   **Expanded Duties Dental Assistant, Dr. William Howard, D.D.S., Dayton, MT**

Jan 1993 - March 1994   **Dental Assistant, Eastern Montana University School of Dentistry, Dayton, MT**

Nov 1991 - Jan 1993   **Chairside Dental Assistant, Dr. Robert Smith, D.D.S., Lafayette, MT**

May 1991 - Sept 1991   **Extern Program, Dr. Richard Spencer, D.D.S., Warren, MT**

EDUCATION/ CERTIFICATION

1992   Graduate, Warren High School, Warren, MT
1990 - 1992   W. G. Wright Career Center, Dayton, MT
- Completed curriculum and certification in dental assisting and maintained an "A" average while completing junior and senior years of high school

HONORS

- Selected as third in the state in dental assisting skills in 1991
- Member of Top Ten in dental assisting skills in the state in 1992

Michael Nasser • 323 Oak Drive • Edenberg, IL • 60016 • (708) 555-3554

Summary of Qualifications

Thorough knowledge of medical terminology, with good understanding of surgical and laboratory procedures. Efficient with WordPerfect and medical transcription software on IBM or compatible system. Ability to type 85 words per minute with high degree of accuracy. Possess necessary equipment and reference materials to work from home. Experienced in medical office management.

Work Experience

Medical Transcriptionist, Columbus General Hospital, Columbus, IL
April 1994 - present
- Transcribe for coronary, neurology, orthopedic, psychiatric and internal medicine physicians in 100-plus physician hospital.
- Evaluated and recommended hiring three part-time transcriptionists to work from their homes instead of hiring two full-time transcriptionists, saving $22,000 annually in wages and benefits.

Office Manager, Hand Surgery Institute, Columbus, IL
May 1992 - April 1994
- Handled payroll, bookkeeping and office scheduling for two surgeons.
- Supervised clinic's insurance clerk, front desk receptionist and part-time transcriptionist.
- Established patient payment plan program, which decreased late payments and uncollectibles by 75%.

Transcriptionist/Coder, Chemical Dependency Center, Crawfordsville, IL
June 1990 - May 1992
- Transcribed medical information for more than 100 patients.
- Assigned international medical procedure codes to patient records for insurance purposes.

Records Clerk, Crawfordsville Medical Clinic, Crawfordsville, IL
June 1989 - June 1990
- Handled documentation, storage and retrieval of medical information for four physicians.
- Assisted with front office/reception duties.
- Evaluated and recommended computerized record keeping; supervised all data entry; resulted in data base that provided easy and quick retrieval of information by patient name, diagnosis, procedure and physician; also helped generate reports for planning and budgeting.

Education

Lincoln Tech Vocational Institute, Peoria, IL (1988-1989)
- Medical transcription
- Medical coding
- Medical terminology

Memberships

National Health Professions Association

Scott Davis

501 N. Jackson Ave.
Akron, CO 80113
(303) 555-9203

Summary of Skills

General
- Perform "C" check maintenance on Boeing 757, Boeing 727 (200 and 100 series aircraft) and L1011 Tristar
- Complete regular 100-hour and annual inspections of aircraft, including Piper Navajo, DC 3, Beech Craft 18 and Cessna 150/180
- Handle regular inspection, compression checks and maintenance of Continental, Lycoming, Pratt and Whitney 1830/2000, and Wright 1820 engines, along with composite repairs

Composite
- Experienced with RB211 core cowls 72-03-01
- Skilled with build-up repair on spoilers on L1011
- Experienced with Honeycomb sandwich repair due to delamination 51-50-07
- Completed the following work on 727:
  - alodine & prime 51-10-2
  - corrosion removal 51-10-6
  - fastener installation 51-30-2
  - typical formed section 51-40-3
  - fiberglass overlays 51-40-8
- Completed the following work on L1011:
  - alodine & prime 51-21-02
  - corrosion removal 51-21-01
  - fastener installation 51-40-00A
  - typical rib or former repair 51-50-03
  - rub strips 51-50-11

Employment History

Airline Maintenance Technician, AmWest Airlines, Denver International Airport, Denver, CO (1993-current)
- Service and handle preventive maintenance on commercial aircraft for regional airline
- Served on team to re-evaluate duties and review maintenance checklist, resulting in new procedures that increased productivity and reduced overlapping responsibilities

Airline Mechanic, Combs Air Maintenance, Denver International Airport, Denver, CO (1991-1993)
- Served as key member of two-man aircraft maintenance and inspection service while attending Lamont University
- Serviced private and corporate aircraft under direct supervision of an A and P certified mechanic

Education

A.S. in Aviation Maintenance Technology, Lamont University (1992)
Additional certification in FAR 65 airframe and power plant mechanics

PATRICK HENNESSEY
1593 Oak St.
Galesburg, Ark. 72847
(501) 555-3922

SUMMARY OF SKILLS

- Skilled in repair and maintenance of automobiles, vans and trucks, with advanced skills in diesel repair and maintenance.
- Strong background in working with cooling, air-conditioning, electrical, fuel, exhaust and steering systems.
- Experienced in tire rotation, rotor resurfacing, bearing replacement and front-end alignment.
- Skilled with all gauges, wrenches, and machine, air and hand tools.
- Experienced in diagnosing performance problems, writing accurate work orders and preparing estimates.

PROFESSIONAL EXPERIENCE

Oct 1993-present **Automotive Mechanic, Goodyear Tire and Repair Service, Galesburg, Ark.**
- Successfully diagnose and repair an average of 10 vehicles per week.
- Handle all diesel repairs.
- Designed new work order form on shop's computer system, resulting in easier access for all mechanics (versus previous manual system where orders could easily be misfiled) and easier retrieval for billing/accounting purposes.

June 1991-Oct 1993 **Automotive Mechanic, Shelby Chevrolet, Hockessin, Ark.**
- Handled repair and maintenance of domestic cars and trucks.
- Ran and maintained the lube rack.
- Recommended use of a new lubricant, which produced superior results at half the cost of previous lubricant.

EDUCATION/ TRAINING

1990 Graduate, Hockessin High School, Hockessin, Ark.
- Related course work: Automotive Shop, Advanced Auto Shop, Computer Operations

1990-1991 Truman Career Vocational College, Waverly, Ark.
- Completed curriculum and certification in automotive repair
- Completed additional certification in diesel repair
- Finished second in graduating class

RELATED INTERESTS
- Build re-creations of vintage sports cars

RONALD G. LAMB
9575 N 450 E
Bismarck, ND 58501
(701) 555-1022

Objective

A carpenter position with a residential builder that provides the opportunity to further develop trim carpentry and electrical wiring skills.

Skills Profile

- Two years experience in residential construction and framework
- Ability to accurately interpret blueprints
- Good background in residential wiring, trim carpentry and crew management
- Experienced in general construction and facility maintenance

Work Experience
March 1994–current

Carpenter Framer and Roofing Crew Manager, Scott Construction, Bismarck, ND
Serve as carpenter framer for residential builder. Construct one-family homes, decks and porches and complete roofing projects on existing homes.
- Manage roofing crew of three, which has completed all assigned residential roofing projects on schedule and on budget.
- Designed 400-square foot home deck and successfully managed construction crew of two.
- Have assisted in trim carpentry on three $250,000+ homes, including crown molding and mantle work.
- Have assisted in two residential wiring projects under supervision of licensed electrician.

June 1992–May 1994

General Laborer, Neese Farms, Inc., Bismarck, ND
Provided general maintenance on farm equipment, out buildings and livestock and grain facilities. Mixed feed and cared for 300-head cattle herd.
- Assisted farm owner in completely re-wiring 100-year-old, two-story house, including removing copper fittings and adding 25 outlets and four ground faults.
- Helped construct 2,500-square foot pole barn and shop area; set frames and supervised pouring of concrete floor and foundation.

Summers 1989–1991

Sales Clerk, Mace Hardware, Bismarck, ND
Handled stocking and helped manage inventory. Completed register sales.
- Recommended new display that better grouped supplies and idea/suggestion sheets for common home projects, saving customers time and extra trips for overlooked supplies; new displays received high customer satisfaction ratings.

Education

Indian Trails High School, Bismarck, ND (1992)

Activities

Making solid oak furniture and scroll saw silhouettes

NATHAN P. ZIMMERMAN
901 Market St.
Jackson, MS 39232
(601) 555-1992

SKILLS SUMMARY

More than 12 years experience in dispatch and driver management. Solid background in scheduling and coordinating delivery dates and times. Good customer relations skills.

WORK EXPERIENCE

Jan 1989-current

Dispatcher, Holden Transit Company, Jackson, MS
Manage dispatching for up to 60 moving van and flatbed drivers.
- Solicit freight from freight brokers, and contact trip lease and port agents to secure flatbed loads.
- Order and procure permits and escorts for over-dimensional, interstate flatbed loads.
- Develop and quote transportation rates to shippers and agents.
- Recommended and implemented new scheduling system, which reduces road hours for drivers and has improved driver safety record.

Aug 1982-Dec 1988

Medical Technician, United States Air Force, Honolulu, HI
Assisted in medical care of sick and injured military patients. Scheduled and trained personnel. Managed equipment, supplies and inventory.
- Supervised Aero Medical Evacuation, including coordinating arrival and delivery dates and times of air evacuation missions with Army and Navy personnel.
- Oversaw conversion of cargo aircraft to air evacuation status, which provided needed medical aircraft while making good use of older aircraft.
- Supervised 20-bed surgical ward.

June 1981-July 1982

Customer Service Representative, Stevenson Lumber, Jackson, MS
Handled customer service requests and inquiries.
- Prepared and coordinated orders for delivery.
- Implemented computerized inventory and delivery system.

EDUCATION

Certificate of Management, Jackson Community College, MS (1993)

CERTIFICATION

Certified Emergency Medical Technician - State of Mississippi

ACTIVITIES

Volunteer, Meyers Memorial Hospital, Jackson, MS

KENT L. McCARTHY
19 E. Walnut St.
Atlanta, Ga. 31113
(404) 555-3343

PROFILE

Skilled manager with more than 10 years experience in defining and achieving organizational performance goals. Able to strategically plan direction of rapidly evolving public safety agency. Adept at designing and implementing innovative management policies, processes and programs.

CAREER HISTORY

Nov 1985-current

Fire Chief, Chief Executive Officer
Center County Fire Department, Atlanta, Ga.
Develop, administer and manage multi-faceted municipal fire department currently employing 160 full-time personnel and serving one of state's rapidly growing, most populous counties. Establish mission and long-range goals, plan objectives and policies, organize human and material resources, direct subordinate chief officers, staff personnel and division managers, and manage $10M annual budget.

- Managed department's transition from volunteer fire department to current status as one of state's 10 largest fire departments.
- Designed and implemented an integrated, state-of-the-art management system with structured and well-defined policies, procedures and processes for recruit selection, performance appraisal, promotion, discipline and more.
- Established system of standard operating procedures that directs and controls all facets of department's emergency operations; one of first in state to successfully implement nationally recognized Incident Command System.
- Designed and implemented Career Development Plan, which provides employees with opportunity to attain career-advancement skills.
- Established one of state's first mandatory physical fitness programs, which has decreased frequency of work-related injuries and increased employees' stamina in hostile environments.

Jan 1990-current

Subcommittee Chairman
Atlanta Hazardous Materials Emergency Planning Committee, Ga.
Chair subcommittee charged with designing and implementing a task force to respond to emergency incidents involving hazardous materials.

- Coordinate and secure commitment from fire, law enforcement, EMS and other public and private sector agencies in three-county area.
- Introduced local ordinances and state legislation regarding emergency plans.

(continued)

CAREER HISTORY
March 1978-Nov 1985

Firefighter/EMT, Paramedic, Company Officer
Fulton County Fire Department, Atlanta, Ga.
- Initiated department's advanced life support program and functioned as liaison officer between department and sponsoring hospital.
- Developed and implemented county's Rescue Diver Training program, which was the first in the tri-county area.
- First to be promoted to company officer after just three years of service.

EDUCATION

National Fire Academy, Emmitsburg, Md. (1988-1991)
- Executive Fire Officer Program

Georgia State University, Atlanta (1977-1978)
- 15 credit hours in management

AWARDS

Community Appreciation for Service in Public Enlightenment and Relations Award, Community Service Council of Northern Georgia (1990)
Community Service Award, Children's Bureau of Atlanta (1992)

PROFESSIONAL CERTIFICATIONS

Master Firefighter - Fire Prevention
Master Firefighter - Tactics
Master Firefighter - Fire Service Management
Master Firefighter - Instructor 1st Class
Master Firefighter - Aircraft Crash and Rescue
Firefighter - First Class
State of Georgia - Emergency Paramedic
State of Georgia - Emergency Medical Technician - Primary Instructor

PROFESSIONAL AFFILIATIONS

International Association of Fire Chiefs
National Fire Protection Association
Georgia Fire Chiefs Association

COMMUNITY ACTIVITIES

Chairman, Aluminum Cans for Burned Children Foundation, Atlanta
Planning Committee, Tri-County Home Safety Program for Children
Volunteer, Burn Unit, Atlanta General Hospital

Greg Timmons

901 East South Street
Bloomfield, MI 48550
(517) 555-6676

Summary of Skills

Generator repair and maintenance	*Can also operate:*
Electric pallet jack repair	Loboy
Freezer maintenance	Forklift
Rapidstand conveyer repair and maintenance	Backhoe
Ammonia systems experience	Bulldozer
Heavy equipment repair and maintenance	Circular saw
Basic residential and commercial construction knowledge	Electric staple gun
Supervisory experience	
Electric drill	

Employment Record

Mitchell's Grocery, Downtown Warehouse, Bloomfield, MI (August 1989-current)
• Work all phases of building maintenance.
• Supervise staff of three on night shift.
• Recommended new preventive maintenance procedure, which reduced machinery downtime and nearly eliminated hourly overtime wages.

Smith and Bright Contractors, Ann Arbor, MI (March 1983-August 1989)
• Managed 25 pieces of equipment and crew of 12.
• Worked on residential and commercial projects.
• Initiated crew rotation schedule, which increased on-time project completion without increasing wage expenses.

Lawrence and Sons Builders, Washington, MI (March 1978-March 1983)
• Provided general labor for residential construction.
• Researched and recommended new roofing product, which provided the high-quality results the builder required at a savings of 20% over the product the builder had used.

Education

Graduate, Truman High School, Applegate, MI (1976)

Military Service

U.S. Army (June 1976 - February 1978)
• Served on construction crew for civil engineering unit

NATALIE W. SANDBERG
5561 Walnut Dr.
Providence, RI 02811
(401) 555-0992

SKILLS SUMMARY

Champion gymnast with five years instructional experience. Adept at assessing students' skills and abilities. Able to develop innovative, age-appropriate curriculum. Solid background in nutritional education.

WORK EXPERIENCE

January 1993-current

Gymnastics Instructor, The Dance Studio, Providence, RI
Develop and teach gymnastics curriculum for preschool students (ages 1-5) at three class levels. Incorporate academic aspect into lessons by using colors, shapes, letters and numbers. Train substitute instructors.
- Established "Moms and Tots" program, which has grown from one class to three classes per week.
- Created "theme" lessons, such as fire safety, the Big Top and football season, which have been adopted by the National Gymnastics Association.
- Organize annual recital, which displays students' progress over the year.
- Coordinated special promotion, which increased number of students 20%.

June 1991-January 1993

Gymnastics Coach, Campbell YMCA, Providence, RI
Instructed 45 students ages 6 to 12. Organized each gymnast according to age and ability into three class levels. Developed and monitored daily workouts and individualized weight training programs.
- Initiated nutritional education through weekly discussions and "mock" training table sessions.
- Coordinated competitive meets, including hiring judges, setting up and inspecting equipment, and securing event runners and awards.
- Placed six students in advanced summer training camps.

Sept 1990-June 1991

Physical Education Teacher/Girls' Volleyball Coach, Walnut Grove High School, Walnut Grove, RI
Developed daily lesson plans and organized classes to help students progress in their physical skills and knowledge of rules for a variety of sports and activities.
- Designed and developed skills tests and written tests for grade levels 9 through 12, which allowed each student opportunity to succeed.
- Coached girls' volleyball team to regional championship.

School year 1989-1990

Gymnastics Instructor, Rhode Island State College, Providence
Taught gymnastics classes offered by college for preschool through high school students. Helped develop preschool curriculum.

EDUCATION/
LICENSING

B.S. in Physical Education, Rhode Island State College, Providence (1990)
Rhode Island State Teaching License (1990)

GYMNASTICS
ACHIEVEMENTS

Women's Gymnastics Team, Rhode Island State College, Providence
- Mental Attitude Award (1988-1990)
- Member, National Qualifying Team (1989)
State Champion, Walnut Grove High School Gymnastics Team (1985, 1986)

Elizabeth Moriarty

62 Eastgate Ct.
Windmere, GA 30998
(404) 555-9023

Summary of Skills

- Experienced in creating innovative programs to involve children in their local library and instill the love of books in children, teachers and parents.
- Skilled in public speaking and communicating information about library programs.
- Thorough knowledge of children's books, reference materials, audio-visual collections and reading/activity computer software.
- Adept in budget management, purchasing and supervising volunteers.
- Strong computer skills.

Professional Experience

Head Librarian, Children's Department, Carnegie Public Library, Windmere, GA
February 1993 - current

Conduct all children's story-telling and special programs. Work with local teachers to help meet instructional needs. Visit local pre-schools, 4-H and Scout meetings and other children's organizations to introduce programs and encourage participation. Order and maintain library collection and track computerized budget.

- Initiated library's bar code system for automated check-out, returns and inventory, resulting in more accurate records, improved inventory and faster check-out/check-in.
- Established Jr. Volunteer program for middle school students to reduce heavy demands on paid staff and introduce students to library operations; volunteers have enhanced operations by reshelving books in a more timely manner, assisting younger patrons with computer skills and helping plan special children's programs.
- Advise student volunteers on Children's Department newsletter, which is distributed to all patrons; newsletter has improved students' computer and communications skills and won recognition from the Georgia Library Association.
- Plan special holiday programs to increase involvement and encourage younger patrons to visit library on regular basis.
- Received library board grant and established children's computer center to enhance computer skills and provide learning opportunity through educational software.

(continued)

Professional Experience

Assistant Librarian, Children's Department, Carnegie Public Library, Windmere, GA
June 1990 - February 1993
- Created children's summer reading program, which nearly doubled the number of young patrons visiting the library.
- Initiated special weekly summer programs, such as arts and crafts, puppet shows, juggling and magic exhibitions, train excursions, author visits, games and music.
- Established weekly Wee Ones story time for 18- to 36-month-old children and Story Time for children ages 3 to 6; after one year, expanded to bi-weekly session to accommodate interested young readers.
- Initiated "Young Puppeteers" for middle-school students, which enhanced their story-telling and creative skills as they presented quarterly puppet shows for elementary-aged children.

Related Experience

Chairman, Children's & Young People's Division, Georgia Library Association
1993-1995
Planned annual fall conference, including researching and hiring speakers and talent, and arranging accommodations and meals. Created and distributed registration/informational brochure.
- Presented session on how to get the most out of youth volunteers without driving them away.
- Initiated "share and compare" session, where attendees exchanged handouts, brochures and flyers to learn about other programming ideas they could use in their own libraries, resulting in more creative programming in all state public libraries.
- Secured corporate sponsor, which reduced registration fees and allowed more members to attend.

Volunteer Librarian, Burrows Elementary School, Windmere, GA
September 1987 - May 1989
Assisted school librarian in reshelving and checking out books and helping students find materials.
- Tutored nearly 20 children in reading.
- Recommended "Book Buddies" program, which enhanced children's literacy by encouraging them to read about a variety of subjects in pairs and present brief reports to their classmates; students won awards based on the number of books read.

Education/Licensing

B.A. in Humanities, Georgia State University, Atlanta (1980)

State of Georgia Children's Specialist License (1992)

Victoria E. Marchetta • 19 Valley Drive • Cleveland, OH • 44101 • (216) 555-2334

Summary of Qualifications

More than 15 years in dance performance, instruction and troupe management. Skilled in developing private dance programs and in managing professional dance theaters, including fund raising, promotions and performance scheduling. Experienced in establishing and administering student scholarship programs and innovative exchange programs.

Professional Experience

Director, Victoria Marchetta School of Dance, Cleveland, OH
(June 1982-present)
Develop and schedule classes, supervise 15 faculty and staff members and manage advertising, public relations, special events coordination and day-to-day-operations. Serve as principal instructor for ballet technique and pointe.

- Maintain state, regional and national reputation for dance program and ability to place students in major dance studios and help students earn scholarships to dance institutions, such as the University of Cincinnati and Julliard.
- Have instructed and placed students with national and international dance companies, such as the Cleveland Ballet, the Dance Theatre of Harlem, the Boston Ballet and the National Ballet of Canada.
- Sponsored and manage liaison program with Cleveland Ballet Theatre, providing instructional experience for young professionals and unique learning experiences for dance students.
- Founded and manage summer scholarship program for dance students.

Artistic Director, Cleveland Ballet Theatre, Cleveland, OH
(March 1990-present)
Manage 50 dancers and artistic staff, setting and staging for ballets, tour coordination, programming and special events.

- Work with development (fund raising), marketing and public relations departments to secure corporate sponsorships of special presentations, which has enhanced troupe's image and increased attendance at all performances.
- Established and secured funding for exchange program with Russian ballet troupe, resulting in once-in-a-lifetime learning experiences for theater members and international performances for theater patrons.

Director, Great Lakes Ballet Ensemble, Cleveland, OH
(January 1987-March 1990)
Managed 30-member company, including tour scheduling, promotions and performance programming.

- Worked with development department to establish special events and fund raisers that recognized and encouraged contributions from individuals, civic and philanthropic organizations and businesses.
- Increased contributions 60% in two years.

(continued)

Professional Experience

Choreographer
(August 1980-present)
Created, arranged and directed dances at a varity of locations, including:
- Victoria Marchetta School of Dance (June 1982-present)
- Cleveland Ballet Theatre (March 1990-present)
- Great Lakes Ballet Ensemble (January 1987-March 1990)
- Cleveland Symphony Orchestra (February 1985-January 1987)
- Cleveland Civic Ballet, Inc. (August 1980-February 1985)

Ballet Mistress, Cleveland Civic Ballet, Inc.
(August 1980-February 1985)
Taught company class to 50 dancers and set and rehearsed ballets.

Performing Experience

Great Lakes Ballet Ensemble (1987-1988)
Cleveland Civic Ballet (1982-1985)
East Lake (Ohio) Summer Theatre (1979-1980)
Ohio University (Athens) Music and Art Camp (Summers 1977-1978)

Education

Markova Dance Studio, New York City, NY (1979)
The Jazz Studio, New York City, NY (1978)
School of American Ballet, New York City, NY (1977-1978)
Morgan Dance Studio, Cuyahoga Falls, OH (1963-1976)
Courses in Performing Arts, University of New York, New York City (1976, 1978)
- 9 credits in dance, 6 credits in performing arts, 12 credits in general studies

Courses Studied

Ballet Technique - Elizabeth Anderson, John Curry, Alexander Dumeo, Nancy Hatfield,
    Talia Markova, Judy Simms, Michael Todd, Guy Charisse
Pointe - Talia Markova, Michael Todd
Pas de Deux - Alexander Dumeo, John Curry
Modern - Judy Simms, Nancy Hatfield
Jazz - Nancy Hatfield, Elizabeth Anderson
Tap - Elizabeth Anderson, Judy Simms
Character - Guy Charisse, Judy Simms
Dance Terminology - Elizabeth Anderson, Nancy Hatfield, Michael Todd

LAURA McINTYRE

1203 Bayview Lane
Sandy Hook, ME 03992

(207) 555-9443 (home)
(207) 555-1002 (work)

SUMMARY OF SKILLS

- Strong background in early childhood care
- Skilled in designing and implementing developmentally appropriate activities
- Able to create and initiate hands-on learning experiences
- Capable of developing nursery school curriculum

EXPERIENCE

1993-present

Day-Care Attendant, The Wonder Years Day Care, Sandy Hook, ME
Provide daily care and attention for children ages 2 to 10 years. Provide safe
transportation for school-age children to and from local elementary school.
- Organize field trips for up to 30 preschoolers to local service agencies, the library
  and other "learning" centers, which introduce children to the world around them
- Initiated use of puppets and water and sand tables for 2- to 3-year olds,
  encouraging creative play and emphasizing hands-on learning
- Initiated morning nursery school program for children not in daily day care, which
  met a community need and enhanced the day-care center's total program
- Assisted manager in creating and teaching nursery school curriculum and related
  activities for up to 15 children each week
- Assisted manager in planning and establishing special summer programs, such as
  swimming, miniature golf, trips to the park and to pick blueberries, and other
  educational and fun experiences
- Assisted manager in converting from manual to computerized bookkeeping, which
  reduced bookkeeping time and produced computerized accounting/tax reports

**Summers
1989-1992**

Child-Care Provider, Sandy Hook, ME
- Ensured fun and safe play environment for three children ages 18 months
  to 5 years
- Prepared snacks and lunches and cleaned up afterward
- Maintained schedule, including naps and outside play time
- Completed light housekeeping duties, such as dishwashing and vacuuming

EDUCATION

Current

Courses toward an Associate's Degree in Early Childhood Education,
    Warsaw Junior College, Warsaw, ME (12 credits, 3.6/4.0 GPA)

1992

Graduate, Sandy Hook High School, Sandy Hook, ME

Christopher A. Galloway

404 E. Main St., Apt. 11B   (918) 555-1221
Winslow, OK 74112

SUMMARY OF SKILLS

- Experienced on-air radio personality with excellent background in creative and technical aspects of radio/sound production.
- Able to adapt to a variety of radio program formats.
- Skilled in developing community involvement programs.

EXPERIENCE

June 1995-present

Disc Jockey, KKKY, Winslow, OK
Handle daily disc jockey responsibilities for 20,000-watt radio station. Deliver public service announcements. Write, produce and provide voice-overs for local commercials. Assist in determining program format.
- Initiated community involvement program with local hospital to offer free health and hearing screenings, which addresses need for quality preventive health care in high-risk population.
- Established fund-raising events on radio air time to benefit Senior Citizens Center and Boys' and Girls' Club, generating nearly $2,000 annually for each group.
- Nominated for Outstanding New Radio Personality by Oklahoma Radio Association.

Owner, Galloway Sound Design, Winslow, OK
Provide sound design consultation and set-up for a variety of clients.
- Manage sound design for Winslow Community School Corporation, including student dances and musical and drama productions.

Sept 1993- June 1995

Disc Jockey/Assistant Station Manager, KCKC, Jacksonville Vocational Community College, OK
Implemented station policies and procedures. Supervised staff of two.
- Introduced new advertising promotion, which increased sales 30%.

EDUCATION

1995

Associate's Degree in Telecommunications, Jacksonville Vocational Community College, OK (3.7/4.0 GPA)

ACTIVITIES

Advisor/Guest Instructor, Vocational Radio/Television Course, Winslow Community School Corporation, Winslow, OK

LESLIE J. TODD

33 River Lane
Cincinnati, Ohio 45287

(513) 555-0922

SUMMARY OF SKILLS

More than 12 years in the interior design business, including specialized experience in restaurant and cafeteria planning and design. Skilled in developing elevations, floor plans and reflected ceiling plans. Strong background in both commercial and residential projects.

WORK EXPERIENCE

May 1993-present

Owner/Designer, L. Todd Interiors, Cincinnati, Ohio
Own and operate interior design company serving residential and commercial customers. Annual sales of $100K. Handle own marketing, purchasing and bookkeeping.
* Began operation from scratch and realized profit after first year.
* Planned office design for–and successfully completed 48-hour relocation of–computer software company, including moving mainframe and computer terminals.
* Provided consultation, design and purchases for two, 200-seat specialty restaurants, including all components of dining area, such as wall cover, flooring, seating, dinnerware and all decorations.
* Supervised $100K home addition, including consultation on construction materials, windows, ceilings, lighting, flooring, furniture and window cover selections.

Sept 1988-May 1993

Designer, Restaurants, Etc., Cincinnati, Ohio
Served as interior designer for company specializing in cafeterias for large office buildings. Produced elevations, floor plans and reflected ceiling plans.
* Provided consultation on materials in kitchen construction, such as walls, floors, ceilings and lighting.
* Planned and purchased all components of dining area, including wall cover, flooring, seating, tables, dinnerware, cutlery and all decorations.
* Planned and supervised $100K food court for shopping mall.
* Designed cafeteria for Justice Center in County Court building.
* Planned and designed interior for $225K, 400-seat restaurant.

(continued)

WORK EXPERIENCE

Jan 1985-Sept 1988	**Designer, Meredith Willing & Co., Cincinnati, Ohio**

One of five designers with privately owned enterprise. Worked with 8 to 10 residential clients annually on a variety of projects ranging from $3-350K. Produced elevations, floor plans and sketches for all projects.
- Determined lighting and selected appropriate fixtures.
- Handled color and fabric schemes and furniture selections.
- Expanded company's client base 25%.
- Helped plan and oversee $350K home addition, including working with the architect and contractor; planned every aspect of interiors for exercise room, children's playroom and in-home bar.

March 1983-Jan 1985 **Purchasing/Contract Specialist, Thomas Interiors, Inc., Cincinnati, Ohio**
Worked for design company with more than 200 commercial clients and $6M in annual sales. Handled correspondence with clients.
- Wrote sales contracts up to $250K.
- Developed price quotes for sales contracts and generated purchase orders for goods and services in contracts.

June 1981-March 1983 **Manufacturer's Manager, The Mart, Cincinnati, Ohio**
Represented 25 manufacturers in showroom. Provided information to– and completed sales with–architects and designers.
- Began as salesperson in retail showroom, promoted to manager after eight months.
- Handled furniture, carpeting and flooring, fabrics and lighting.

EDUCATION

June 1981 Bachelor's Degree in Fine Arts, University of Cincinnati, Ohio
Major: Interior Design
Minors: Ceramics, Drawing

AFFILIATIONS

1987-present Member, American Society of Interior Designers
1992-present Director, Greater Cincinnati Home-A-Rama Showcase

```
┌─────────────────────────────────┐
│      Cosmetologist/Salon Manager │
│            Chronological         │
└─────────────────────────────────┘
```

Jamie Calahan

> 1053 Alamo Way, Apt. 3B
> Austin, TX 78788
> (512) 555-9340

Summary of Skills

> Licensed cosmetologist with 12 years experience in styling, training and management. Ability to successfully develop and implement special sales promotions. Strong customer service, purchasing and inventory background.

Product Experience

> Shampoos–Redken, Nexxus, Matrix, Paul Mitchell, Sebastian, Image, Malibu 2000, Clairol, Brocato
> Perms–Redken, Matrix, Nexxus, Helen Curtis, Revlon, Zotos
> Color–Redken, Matrix, Sebastian, Framesi, Sunglitz, Goldwell
> Nails–OPI, Creative Nail, Solar Nail

Training Experience

> Assistant Redken Deco Color Trainer (1983-86)
> Sunglitz Technical Trainer (1990-91)
> OPI Nail Trainer (1988-1990)
> Helene Curtis Perm Specialist (1987-1989)

Work Experience

Manager, Cut-ups Hair Salon, Austin, TX (1991-current)
- Operate salon under corporate policies, hire and train employees, handle payroll and manage purchasing and inventory
- Handle and address customer service problems
- Initiated money-back guarantee program for four local stores, which increased monthly sales by $2,000

Senior Stylist/Nail Technician, Macey Company, Austin, TX (1987-1991)
- Handled purchasing, inventory, cutting, coloring, perming and styling for major department store chain salon
- Served as team training leader and trained all new stylists
- Recommended and implemented special services and equipment for handicapped customers at local store; program won local acclaim, increased sales and was implemented in other company salons throughout the state

Stylist/Assistant Manager, Hair By Design, Gateway, TX (1983-1987)
- Began as stylist; promoted to assistant manager after one year
- Handled product orders, customer service, inventory and all cosmetology services
- Created special Mother's Day gift certificate promotion, which resulted in 14 new permanent customers for private salon

Licensing

> Anthony's Cosmetology College, Austin, TX (1983, Licensed Cosmetologist)

Resume index and cross-reference

Situational resumes

Occupational resumes